PROBLEM
DOG

JANICE R. OTTER, MIPBC

AuthorHouse™ UK
1663 Liberty Drive
Bloomington, IN 47403 USA
www.authorhouse.co.uk
UK TFN: 0800 0148641 (Toll Free inside the UK)
UK Local: 02036 956322 (+44 20 3695 6322 from outside the UK)

This book is printed on acid-free paper.

ISBN: 979-8-8230-8397-3 (sc)
       979-8-8230-8398-0 (e)

Library of Congress Control Number: 2023913819

Print information available on the last page.

Published by AuthorHouse 08/02/2023

authorHOUSE®

Janice R Otter MIPBC is a Pet Behaviourist with over 25 years of experience. She has saved thousands of dogs from being destroyed and trained hundreds of owners.

To my loving husband Michael,
for his patience and understanding.

To my lovely daughter
Jocelyn – where would I be without her, and her technical wizardry!

Also to my friend Sue Riley,
without whom this book would never have come together.

I would like to dedicate this book to Billy a real heart breaker.

ACKNOWLEDGEMENTS

A big thank you to Steve Kemp for his illustrations and book cover.

CONTENTS

INTRODUCTION
HOW THE DOG THINKS

Another news bulletin or newspaper report and another person or child has been mauled or worse, killed, by either their own pet dog or their neighbour's or family friend's dog.

In the past, dog attacks did not happen as frequently as today. Dogs today are a very popular companion, but unfortunately man's best friend is rapidly becoming public enemy number one. But why? Literature and television programmes on how to train dogs being plentiful, one would expect all dogs to be perfectly trained, but they are not.

Understanding a dog is paramount in being able to train it. You need to know when the dog does something out of the ordinary how to cope, understand why the dog has done what it has, and be capable of correcting the problem without the use of bribery or aversion methods of any kind. These alone can cause problems.

Firstly, all dogs learn by association. All dog behaviour is learnt, the second they enter our lives even at the tender age of eight weeks old, the only information the dog has is what nature provided and what follows is down to us.

Working with dogs with behavioural problems for over twenty years, I understand the usual problems faced by owners every day. For example, the dog growls at the owner, snaps at the children, urinates on the furniture, on walks it is intent on fighting every dog it encounters, and when released from the lead it will not heed when called. All of the aforementioned can be remedied.

The general consensus of opinion is that the dog's evolution through the years is firmly connected to the wolf, but knowing about the wolf will only hinder rather than help you. It is not the wolf in the dog that is the problem. Wolves have nothing to do with your dog's behaviour, your problems are man-made. Therefore, if you wish to read about wolves then this is not the book for you.

The famous Russian Physiologist, Ivan Petrovich Pavlov, who was born in 1849, made a great breakthrough when he discovered "Conditional Reflexes". By simply ringing a bell, the dogs reacted to the sound of the bell and he fed them. Therefore, from then onwards each time the dogs heard the sound of the bell they would associate this with being fed and would salivate with anticipation. Another familiar conditional reflex is when a dog is put in a room and the door is closed. If the dog resents being left in the room it may start to scratch at the door to be let out. Your first instinct would be to save the door from further damage, so open it, problem solved. The dog's problem is also solved. Once the door is open the dog is happy as it did not want to be in the room, therefore it will know what to do for the door to be opened in the future.

Now you have a brief but informative insight into how your dog thinks – please read on.

CHAPTER 1
PUPPIES

Puppies are not toys, they do not respond favourably in the long run to being picked up and cuddled or carried around, especially by children.

Children are the losers between man and dog, simply because they see the dog as a plaything and the dog sees the child as someone to dominate, and we all know the consequences of that particular combination.

The first thing we need to teach the puppy is its name and the word "no". In the beginning, what we need to know about the puppy is that it learns by association, which means it reads our reaction and how we responded to whatever the puppy gets up to.

Puppies are like children, apart from the obvious bits. We do not speak the same language but we communicate in the same way. They step out of line and we call them by their name to get their attention and then we say "no".

All dog breeds are the same when it comes to learning, even if the dog is deaf. No breed is different or any more difficult to teach than the next. It is how we teach them that makes the difference. If we teach the dog the wrong information, then all we receive is misunderstandings, which in turn leads to problems. If we get it right then the rewards are immeasurable. (To the younger reader this means "wicked"!) The main aim that everyone wants from their dog is respect, once this is achieved man and his best friend will truly get on together.

The perfect age for a puppy to be taken home is eight weeks. This is the right age for it to accept noises of the household. Problems are found with puppies if they are taken away too early or too late.

If a puppy has been brought up in a house it will already be used to the sounds of washing machines, vacuum cleaners, televisions and children squealing and shouting. If the puppy was brought up outside away from these everyday sounds then it is down to the owner to acclimatise the puppy in a responsible way.

The next important thing we need to know is that regardless of its age, the second the dog steps over the threshold it will have its own agenda. It will join our pack with the pack mentality, and if the opportunity allows it to rule the roost, then rule the roost it will.

Therefore the puppy needs to know its boundaries the moment it walks through the door. It is not essential that the puppy has a cage; cages are big and inconvenient and once the puppy is used to it, you then have to get it unused to it. We only use them because we fear the dog will destroy our home by chewing or messing everywhere, but if you get the training right you will never experience any of these problems.

The puppy should have its own place to sleep; this is usually in the kitchen, never anywhere else, definitely not in the bedroom. Some dog training books advise putting the puppy in your bedroom until it gets used to being away from its mother – this is not a good idea. It will get used to it and not want to come out and will react badly at night when you do leave it in the kitchen. So start as you mean to go on, the sooner the puppy gets used to being on its own the better it will cope. Ignore all the noises the puppy makes, never come down at night or it will always expect you to.

House training a puppy is relatively simple if you know what you are doing. This task should be completed between the ages of twelve to sixteen weeks old. Do not make the mistake of believing that the puppy will not mess in the house at night just because it is house trained by day. When nature runs its course the puppy will be able to go through the night.

When you are not present, cover the floor with newspapers so when the puppy goes willy nilly as it will, the cleaning up will be easier. Do not spend money on fancy training pads; paper is just as effective (and cheaper). There is enough expense anyway without adding to it.

When you are there with the puppy you need to keep it in the same room as yourself and keep the door closed if possible. Do not let the puppy roam around the house, if you do it will mess anywhere it likes. If you are in the kitchen, for example, keep the puppy there with you and keep an eye on it and as it crouches down to do something, do not shout or frighten it, just put your finger through the collar and coax it outside, saying "outside" as you go. If your puppy is deaf do exactly the same motion but at the same time get the puppy's attention by getting eye contact, and using a sign, for example, pointing to the door it is to go through, any sign you are comfortable with is acceptable but remember everyone must use the same sign.

Do not, as some puppy training books advise, pick it up and take it out and wait with it and then praise it when it has done something. Two problems arise here, the first one is if you praise the puppy for doing something outside, then tell it off when it does it inside; this will only confuse the puppy. It does not understand the difference – it only knows that it has been to the toilet.

The second problem is, because puppies learn by association it will naturally presume that every time it needs to go out it will get picked up. Also to finalise the house training section, a dog is more likely to want to go out after it has been asleep, not long after a meal and after playing. Some books suggest you let them out at these times. Do not. Just be aware after these activities and wait until the puppy shows signs of wanting to go. If you start to second guess then you will always be doing it.

It is now that the puppy starts to learn, but their attention span is limited, so teaching the puppy little but often will pay in the end. It is at this stage they need to socialise with people, traffic, other dogs, noises, babies and children, indeed everything that they will normally encounter in their everyday lives. Be careful how you handle this stage, it is a time when anything frightening or traumatic will have a lasting impression on the puppy.

Always be aware of the behaviour of children, they can sometimes be a little rough and then the puppy will be wary of children, which is the last thing we want. The puppy should not be constantly pestered when it is asleep; they are like babies and need their sleep. This is when the puppy's easy going temperament turns it into a nasty disagreeable dog.

When you have your training sessions, do not shout or lose your temper. It will be preferable if you have a bed time for the puppy, perhaps one hour before you go to bed, this will give you some peace for yourself.

Punishment – this is to be a consequence for the puppy not reacting to a command. The puppy decides it is going to arrange your flowers on the hearth; the first thing to do is to send a warning shot across the bows by calling the puppy's name and saying "no". If it continues the second time you say "no" you take the puppy away from the family unit and put it in a room on its own. This room is usually the kitchen. Leave the puppy for ten minutes only and only let it out when it is quiet, and not before. After ten minutes, let it out without speaking to it and then go back in the room and if it goes to the same place again to continue where it left off, you repeat the command as before and if it disobeys again it's back to the kitchen. As we now know how the puppy learns, it will soon realise that flower arranging constitutes a spell in solitary confinement!

If your puppy is deaf and decides to misbehave, you go to hold its head to get eye contact and using a sign that means "no", repeat exactly as for a hearing puppy.

Teething always causes problems; the puppy will have a go at anything to relieve the need to chew. He needs something cold and hard, similar to a teething ring we would buy for a baby, you can buy these aids in a pet shop. Biting also comes with teething, biting hands, trouser legs, hanging on to the bottom of dressing gowns as you walk pass. This is where punishment comes into play – what the puppy thinks is a good game is a very dangerous pastime and needs stopping or it could turn into something more sinister.

All puppies have a mad half hour, where they will run up and down and around the house then flop down (thankfully) and go to sleep. This, funnily enough, is normal. Only if the puppy starts to snap at people as it runs by should you put it outside to let it release some of its energy. This activity will last until the puppy is around a year or so but will happen less frequently as the puppy grows up.

To teach the puppy to sit, lay and stay in that order; put the puppy in the sitting position then gently place your hand on its back end and push it down until it is in the sitting position. As you do this say "sit" and then praise the puppy. Next make it sit, then scoop its front paws forward while you push down gently on its shoulders until it is in the lying position saying "lay down" at the same time, then praise it. The next thing to teach is to stay, and when it has, even if it has only been for a second you praise it. I have found over the years, it is very useful to use hand signals for each command you give your dog, this way in the future, there will be no need for words, hand signals are all you need. Repeat these exercises but do not overdo it.

To teach a deaf puppy to do these things is just as easy providing you get the signs across to the dog without making it complicated. You want it to sit, make the sign and put it in the position and over fuss it but not for too long. If you want the puppy to come to you, find a sign that attracts the puppy, for example, waving your arms in the air and then really fuss it when it comes to you. Do not use treats to get what you want; it will not work out in the end.

Remember the punishment is still the same. Do not be fooled into being too soft, they still have the same intention and the same capabilities as a hearing puppy.

Feeding your puppy – make it sit and stay, put the bowl down, then let the dog know it is allowed to go and eat, Whilst it is eating, stroke it several times, there is no need for fancy footwork when it comes to getting the puppy used to being touched. Some dog books recommend you pick the bowl up and pretend to eat from it; there is no reason why you should. The same is said about eating your meal before the puppy has its meal; there is no need to go to such lengths. Whether the puppy eats before you or after has no relevance as long as discipline is in place. Always feed the puppy in a busy area even if it is a busy time so it gets used to traffic around when it is eating.

If you give your puppy treats (not rewards), offer the treat to the puppy and be aware it might snatch, so be ready if it does so you can quickly withdraw your hand and say "no", offer the treat again and repeat until it takes it nicely.

Play should always be constructive, never rough and tumble on the floor. Ball games – teach the puppy to retrieve by throwing the ball and encourage it to bring it to you. Tugging games are another source of entertainment. Always make sure that when the game is over you are the one that not only ends the game but you end the game the winner. Do not let the puppy run off with the trophy; you decide when the game is over simply by putting the toy on the floor and walking away. The reasoning behind this is that we see it as a game but the puppy sees it as a challenge.

Always make sure the puppy has plenty of toys, they should always have something of their own to play with. They should be able to amuse themselves, it is the same as giving a child a colouring book whilst you get on with other things, and they do not need our constant attention. If the puppy takes something that does not belong to it, take it away and replace it with a toy of its own, if this fails it's punishment time.

If you go to work and need to leave the puppy then do so... they need to get used to being left so they will be able to cope on their own. The moment the puppy steps into our home it must learn that life does not revolve around it. At eight weeks a puppy needs to be left for short periods at a time, the older it gets the longer it can be left. If you can pop back at lunch time or get a friend or family member to go round and let it out this would be a great help. But at some point you will have to cut the apron strings and allow the puppy to manage on its own. This is usually, in my opinion, around five months old.

If you intend to take the puppy out in the car you need to do it from the beginning so it becomes second nature, otherwise you could be in for tough time. Whatever you need your dog to get used to, now is the time to do it.

Walking – teaching the puppy to walk properly is the most simplest of tasks. If you are starting with a puppy for the first time, you are starting with a blank slate but yet we always seem to make a mess of it and spend good money to be taught how to do it. Firstly, forget putting the puppy on a long flexible lead, this is the downfall of nearly all walking problems. I have mentioned from the beginning how the dog learns, so by putting it on the end of a very long lead out in front of you, then at the end of a very long lead out in front is where the dog will expect to be. Start with a short lead holding it with your left hand, enough to let the puppy put its nose to the ground. The rest of the lead should be held in your right hand stopping the puppy from walking from side to side in front of you. With the puppy on your left side make it sit, then walk forward. If the puppy walks in

front of you, stop and bring it back to your side, using whatever word or sign you are comfortable with. Repeat the process until the puppy no longer steps in front of you.

Puppies do not know what a lead is; they do not understand the concept of being attached to the end of a lead because up until now they have been able to run freely. Therefore you will find that taking the puppy for a walk for the first time is not as simple as you thought it might be. Some will bite the lead, some will rear up and some will not walk at all, they will park their bum firmly on the pavement and totally refuse to move. If you hold the lead correctly you will stop the first two, as for the (bum firmly on the pavement) protest you simply pull the puppy along coaxing it as you go until it get the message, giving in to it at this early stage is not the thing to do.

Puppies are very vulnerable when they are on the toilet, sleeping and eating. These are the times when the puppy's guard is down. You will probably find that when you are out walking, the puppy will not do its toilet until you get home. If you have taken your puppy out and it has failed to do anything, do not, when you return home, take the dog straight indoors, leave it in the garden where it feels safe to do it. You will find, however, that as it gets older it will do it on walks.

Other little idiosyncrasies that puppies get up to is eating poo. To stop this do not clean up the garden until you have let the puppy out, like all misdemeanours you have to catch them red-handed to make the crime stick. So follow the puppy into the garden to see what it does, if it goes up to the poo and smells it (like dogs do) that is alright. If it tries to eat it, then you say "no". The puppy should walk away, if it does not and goes to eat it, then it is punishment time. Do the same thing if it humps cushions or legs.

Puppies have two fright stages. One is when we first take it home and it gets used to household noises and training methods – these, as we know, should be handled with care. The second one occurs around the age of eight months onwards. For example, we are out with the puppy and we come across a wheelie bin on the pavement, the puppy will, when young, approach the bin with caution, it will slowly but surely go up to the bin check it out and unless the bin moves on its own or says "boo", the puppy will accept it, sniff and walk on. We do nothing, even if the puppy sidles past showing fear it is up to the puppy to come to terms with it, we do not interfere. The same outcome if another dog approaches and wants to have a sniff at the puppy. That is fine, if it runs behind us for protection we still do nothing, unless of course the other dog is nasty then we step in to protect our puppy.

This is the adolescent puppy, it can be nervous towards something different or a new fear towards the familiar. Be kind and patient; do not force your puppy into situations which might cause stress.

It is also the time when the puppy will push the boundaries, where it thinks it knows it all and quite capable of handling anything, whether it is running after a bird across the fields or it decides it is not coming in from the garden when called, they think it cool until someone lets off a firework or a thunder storm rears its ugly head. This sorts the men from the boys. Some react to the sounds and some do not. The moment the puppy reacts to the noise you totally ignore it and get on with what you are doing. Do not turn up the television or anything else to drown out the noise. If the puppy comes to you for protection you blank it. The second you shown any concern whatsoever by trying to comfort the puppy; you will be submitting your puppy to a life of anxiety.

Throughout this chapter all training is done by being firm but fair. If everyone followed these instructions to the letter, I would be out of a job, but better still, all dog shelters would be empty.

CASE HISTORY ONE
PUPPIES

When I was young life, was good. Very little stopped me from enjoying life. I was, to a certain extent allowed "my head" as they say, but obviously there were times, like most of us, when we are reined in at some point and made to toe the line.

Most problems which would give me grief would usually emanate from the lack of understanding and to my relief the problems were mostly spirited away by the people who loved me the most.

I remember lying in my bed on a hot summer's night, flitting in and out of sleep, the heat of the day had dragged interminably into the night. The night was very dark, it was moonless, not even a slight breeze which would give the illusion that it might improve, the night was airless and everywhere was still.

It was a familiar sound which attracted my attention. I caught my breath and held it for what seemed a very long time. I thought I had heard in the distance the low rumbling sound of an approaching thunderstorm. I listened carefully, and, yes I was right, I had heard thunder and I also knew, through experience, it would not be in the distance for much longer, it was on its way.

I was frightened, I knew it would crash with ear splitting intensity, with bright jagged lights which would light up the night sky as if mimicking daylight, and then plunge me back into darkness.

I started to stress and then I panicked. I leapt from my basket and ran wildly to the door, scratching until my paws bled, howling and screaming for someone to come and help me, because I knew what was outside was beating its way into the house to get at me.

What a reaction – for something to revert to such lengths through fear, is the stuff of nightmares, but at least we wake from our nightmares. What you have just read is, without doubt, one of the most horrendous things that anyone can witness.

Astraphobia is the fear of thunderstorms. It is a very frightening experience for anyone who suffers from it, but this is what people put their dogs through. They do not realise the dangers of subjecting a dog to what is initially a human error, and then it all snowballs. Where people are concerned you can reason with them and explain to them what is actually happening, but when you inflict your worries and insecurities on to someone or something else it is not acceptable, especially when it is a young animal, and then call it love.

Had the dog been left to its own innocence it would have come to terms with it. Thunderstorms have been around for thousands of years. We do not take on board the fact that a dog is not human. The dog looks nothing like us, it does not walk like us and it does not even talk the same language. So why do we get on so well? Because the dog trusts us and we sometimes get it wrong. Ouch, I've just fallen off my soap box!

CASE HISTORY TWO
PUPPIES

Question One

As puppies are constantly growing up, their training also alters according to their age. When they are very young the training is not as intense because their attention span is limited, so spending hours trying to train the pup to do something particular is a waste of time and effort. But there are certain things you can and must introduce to your puppy training as soon as possible.

To help with this I will start by covering the most common questions people ask when they have a puppy.

The most popular question asked is – I cannot house train my puppy. I have tried everything. I have read all the books and watched all the television programmes and logged on to the internet and still I cannot get it right, where am I going wrong?

Here I must sympathise with the owners, the world and his wife have an opinion on this one. My first question is – how old is the dog? This is a very important point, because far too many people expect far too much too soon.

House training is one problem I can advise about over the phone and do on a regular basis. For an adult dog I always ask them if the house training is not put to rights in a week they are to give me another ring. (They never do!).

The answer to this problem is in the question. There is too much conflicting information and people get bogged down with it. House training is one of the simplest things you can train a dog to do (at any age). The puppy is half taught by nature and the rest is up to us. Follow this in the Puppies Chapter, it's foolproof.

Question Two

Why does my dog jump up?

Dogs jump up because they are taught at a very early age. The puppy soon learns that if I do this, this happens. So when the puppy is about eight weeks old and it jumps up and only reaches your ankle, it gets a cuddle, in some cases it gets lifted up in the arms of a loving owner.

We all know that puppies grow quicker than our bank balance, so by the time it gets to chest height and we have been bounced off the wall for the umpteenth time, we know things have gone too far.

This leads to another question about jumping up, which is, why does my dog jump up at people in the street? The answer is simple, dogs treat people in the same way, regardless of whether it is outdoors or indoors.

Question Three

When I take my dog out or even if it is in the garden, when it has been to the toilet it will use its back legs to scrape all the dirt and half my lawn (a slight exaggeration in my view), to cover over where it has been. Why does it do that?

This question leads neatly into another question that is often asked. Whilst they are out walking why does the dog roll in every obnoxious substance that it finds along the way? We get fed up with bathing the dog when we get home.

These two actions from the dog are connected. There used to be a time when a dog was a dog. It would hunt for its food and in turn used to be hunted. It would know the value of life and how to maintain it. It did not always lie on a soft feather bed and have a pretty pink coat or a diamond collar around its neck. It had a family to keep safe and a territory to protect.

To answer the first question, the dog is covering up its toilet smells so the animal who is trailing it is put off tracking him because he has covered his scent, and by using the same mentality it would roll in another animal's excrement to leave a different animal scent altogether. So when the hunter thinks it is following a dog it is actually following a load of bull!

Dogs have a natural instinct that we either know about or do not care about, but either way it still exists and the reason why we keep dogs these days are far removed from the reasons our predecessors kept them. Whether we like it or not the dog's instinct will outrank our idiosyncrasies every time.

Question Four

Another common question asked is – how can cats and dogs get on together? All the dogs I know chase cats every time they set eyes on them. Or they will say, we have cats and I really want a dog as well but they do not mix.

There are two answers to this question on how to cope. The first one is that puppies, as we all know, like to chase anything that moves, even a leaf blowing in the wind, the puppy will run after it, it is a natural reaction.

Puppies are so innocent and do not know any better, they see a constant stream of fun and games, something to eat and with a quick nap in between they are off again. To introduce a puppy to cats is a simple thing to do, providing the cat has an escape route it will cope very well. Once the cat or cats have sussed out the opposition they can take it or leave it. A puppy is no threat to them, so nine times out of ten they tend to take it and a good relationship often develops.

On the other hand if you have a dog from a shelter then the likelihood of it responding favourably to a cat is slim. So in this case you need total control over your dog to affect any friendliness between them. Putting them in the same room together, hoping they will come out bosom buddies (with or without an escape plan), is not going to work. In these circumstances it is important you have your recent acquisition (another word for you kids to look up) spot on in the discipline stakes.

Just a quick note for anyone who is thinking of buying a dog when they already have a cat, you should be aware that cats can be jealous animals, especially when they see love and affection which used to be all theirs directed to the enemy in the camp. Their cute little noses can soon feel pushed out. The consequences of this can be that the cat leaves home.

I have been asked to resolve this particular problem many times over the years, not to sort out the dog but to reunite owners and their cats. Before this problem gets out of hand always make sure you give your cat extra time out to play games and extra cuddles. Park the dog up in another room and give the cat some quality time.

CHAPTER 2
USE OF CAGES

I get quite worried when I see an advertisement for dog cages and read, and I quote, "Always remove leash and collar before allowing pet to enter a pen, cage or crate".

More and more people are using cages to put their dogs in and there are inherently some long lasting consequences. Cages are a convenient cop-out for people who cannot cope with their dog and find a totally inapt excuse for putting them in one. Most of the time the cage is used incorrectly because the owners do not have a clue, and having a clue is paramount to dog owning.

The number of times I have heard people say that they are crate training their dog, "crate training"! What is that about? People actually train their dogs to go into these contraptions. I am not opposed to them totally, they can be very useful, some dogs will benefit from them for a short period of time, especially if your dog is suffering from over-bonding, and this can be explained in Chapter 6, but should not be used as a quick fix for every problem under the sun. For example, where house training is concerned some owners do, especially with puppies, go out and buy a cage and when the going gets tough they put the puppy into it and hope for the best. Some people have openly admitted to knowing that dogs do not mess in their own beds and that is why they put them in there when they cannot cope, and imagine their surprise; when a puppy needs to go, it will go.

Chewing is another reason pets are caged. This is one of the most popular unacceptable things a dog finds itself behind bars for. Chewing is not, and I repeat not, a trait associated with any particular breed of dog. All dogs chew, it is why they do it that we need to understand and then we can do something about it. There are two reasons why a dog would munch on our worldly goods. One is if you have a puppy and chewing is natural when it is teething. The second, if the dog has over bonded and the chewing takes on a different meaning but not the popular conception everyone seems to think, which is that the dog is bored. Dogs do not get bored, that is a human trait. A well balanced dog would be quite happy to while away the time until the family returns home. You will discover what causes this problem in Chapter 6 – Over-bonding.

Some people believe that a dog needs its own space, alone and away from the rest of the family and so they purchase a cage purposely for this particular usage; why this is not a good idea, take a gander at Chapter 5.

Another good reason for not using the cage is if you have a boisterous dominant dog, then you should never leave an undisciplined dog in a cage. These are the ones, when left, will chew a door jamb or two and wreck doors by constantly scratching and attacking them. If you were to put the same individual into a cage its reaction would be disastrous and so much damage would be done, it makes a mockery of the manufacturers warning. If you were to loosely compare the two, for example, the over-bonded dog would chew at mats and anything else lying about, the dominant dog would obliterate them.

The cage is not a magic box where you put your dog into and it comes out cured – the reality is quite the opposite, you are, metaphorically speaking, sweeping your troubles under the carpet.

CASE HISTORY - ONE
USE OF CAGES

I received a call one evening from a very distressed gentleman.

"Hello, sorry to ring so late, we've just arrived back from the vets. We have had to take our dog, Brandy, there, he is in a right mess," he paused, "Oh, sorry, my name is Mr Roberts and I think I had better start from the beginning."

"We have had Brandy, a Weimaraner, from a pup and somewhere along the line I think we have come off the rails with him, or there is something radically wrong. We cannot cope with his behaviour," he said, sounding very despondent.

I was very much in the dark as to what had befallen Brandy, but I did get the feeling that Mr Roberts was not a very happy person. I have learnt over the years to listen to people's obvious distress because I know it helps them to get it off their chest and I learn a lot about what has happened and why. It is when the tirade is over I can make an informed diagnosis and reassure them that all is not lost.

"Brandy is a very difficult and obstinate dog, he has a mind of his own and will not obey if he decides he doesn't want to," he said. "When we leave him to go out to work he just wrecks the house and has destroyed the back door. He has cost us thousands of pounds, but because we love him and we need to save our home we bought a cage," he paused, as if waiting for a reaction, he did not get one because it was at that point I realised why Brandy had snapped! And I could have told Mr Roberts his reason for visiting the vets but that is not my style.

"We arrived home this evening and the cage is a twisted mangled mess. Brandy was loose, bleeding from his paws and mouth so we rushed him to the vets," he said. "The vet has attended his wounds and he will recover. They have done their bit and suggest Brandy's problems are of a behavioural nature and that is why I have telephoned you," he concluded.

If a dog reacts this badly to being left in the house alone and causes damage to such an extent, what makes any right minded person think that putting their dog in a cage will make it better. The answer to that is a person who does not understand dogs as well as they thought. We are not the only thinking animal on this planet, so give a thought for the others, think dog for a change.

CASE HISTORY TWO
USE OF CAGES

I was asked to visit Mr and Mrs Anderson; they were having trouble with their puppy. The couple were having a rough time of understanding the puppy. They have had dogs, from puppies, all their lives and their last dog died at the ripe old age of fourteen. Therefore, they thought they would buy another puppy.

They were now much older and settled in their ways, the house was just the way they wanted it, new carpet, new three piece suite etc. and now these things were in place they were hopefully going to see them into their dotage. Unfortunately, they had forgotten how much a puppy needs training and how messy they could be. So although they had never used a cage for any of their other dogs, it was time to go out and buy one.

Because of their insecurities, they used the cage incorrectly. When I visited the Andersons, the puppy had spent most of its young life in the cage. When Mrs Anderson allowed the puppy into the living room it would run amok everywhere, on furniture, side tables, even trying to climb on to the window sill, and would pause only to attack something or urinate on the carpet. Mrs Anderson could never settle to watch TV so the dog was banished out of the sitting room and into the secure wing, i.e. the kitchen and then into the cage.

Mrs Anderson could not cope with this highly energetic puppy. The cage was in the kitchen and she would allow the puppy to roam around whilst she was there but whenever she wanted to leave the room the puppy wanted to follow, so to avoid tussling in the doorway every time she left the kitchen, she would put the puppy in the cage. If she did not go in willingly (which was on a regular basis), she would throw a treat into the cage and then quickly close the door. Mrs Anderson also had a problem house training, as she would take the puppy outside and stand with it to be sure it did something. There were times when she had to rush the puppy for various reasons, and would not stop with it very long and take the puppy back indoors. Because she was not sure whether she had done her toileting Mrs Anderson would put her in the cage to be on the safe side and to save her kitchen floor. What the puppy really wanted to do was romp around the garden exploring every crevice, taking in all the smells and discovering new things and thoroughly enjoying herself.

I had to convince Mrs Anderson that she was wrong in what she was doing. I had to make her understand that the only way to do this was for her to sacrifice something for a short period of time to get the puppy on the right track. She did not seem to realise the puppy acted the way it did in the sitting room because it did not know any better. How can a dog respect the rules of the house if it does not know what they are? It has to be taught how to behave correctly. There is no point in owning a dog if you are going to keep it in a cage. It had been a long time since the Anderson's had a puppy and we all tend to get it wrong now and again and plump for the easy option.

The puppy is now a happy, thriving little individual and never misses an episode of Corrie!

CHAPTER 3
AGGRESSION TOWARDS OTHER DOGS

Aggression between dogs is common; it is one of the most common complaints which I receive. The explanation for this is simple. Dogs used to get on alright until we intervened and started to change things to suit ourselves.

Dogs are not naturally aggressive towards their own kind, they are after all pack animals and if aggression was the norm they would be extinct by now. There are two main reasons why a dog would fall out with another dog.

One, if the dog was not properly socialised at the right age, and two, if the dog has been attacked or badly frightened by another dog at some point in its life; if this has happened then they will be very wary of meeting other dogs in case they get attacked again. Therefore, following this mentality a dog will go two ways; either it will cower or show other submissive tendencies which would be expected from a low ranking dog, or a dog might go on the attack, which as we all know is the best form of defence, which is synonymous (dictionary time for you

youngsters!) with the middle and the high ranking dog. Some high ranking dogs will take no nonsense from the other dogs and no notice of its owner and go in for the kill. A dog has to have been badly brought up for this to happen. Real aggression in dogs is rare, for the reasons I have mentioned. Some dogs will try to bite the owner's hand which is holding the lead so it can get to its quarry.

Dogs do not wake up one morning and think, "I am going to attack the next dog I see." All actions a dog takes in its life are learnt. Dogs are all born equal; it is how life treats them that make them what they are. They come into this life unadulterated and ready for the world to make its mark and it is at this point that we either get it right or wrong.

Therefore we will work on the assumption that we have got it wrong. We are walking the dog down the street and it reacts badly to another dog we meet. What do we do? Firstly, we reel in the dog and as soon as we have done that the dog is suddenly aware and so it starts to look for the reason why and is now on its guard that is always providing we have clocked the other dog first. That is obviously mistake number one. If your dog is walking by your side, as it should be, and not in front on a flexi lead, you do not need to waste time hauling the dog towards you; usually by now you are far too late. Or when you see the other dog coming you try to make your dog sit and calm it down by stroking and giving soothing words of comfort. What you are actually doing is condoning your dog's bad behaviour. As far as the dog is concerned he thinks he is doing a good job and you are pleased with him. The main thing to do here is to keep walking.

Do not follow what the majority of my clients do when they have a problem like this "I do what I see on the television, either when I get near to the other dog I turn round and walk back the other way, or I will take my bottle of pebbles and shake it at the dog to distract it." I cannot for the life of me understand how either of these two actions will cure a dog of aggressive behaviour. It is as effective as finding a burglar in your home and shaking your pebbles at him! This is a serious business, it is not a game, someone could get hurt and not only your dog.

Some dogs are bullies and are quite capable of bullying other dogs in the street. If a high ranking dog meets a lower ranking dog it will try and pull towards it, barking and grumbling, meaning that when it does this in the street the owner cannot stop it from happening. People will say to me, "He does not have a go at every dog he sees, some dogs he ignores." This is typical of a bully, it spies a higher rank that itself and keeps a low profile, but even so it is a show of aggression and it needs to be stopped.

Once you have mastered Chapter 11 – Discipline, you can go out and reunite your dog with the rest of the canine world. The task now is to get your dog to interact with other dogs, but this time you are at the helm, you are in control and not the dog. If you have succeeded in getting him to listen to every word you say you should be able to walk down the street and even if there is another dog coming the other way, you know what your dog is capable of doing. When he sees the other dog just remind him by saying "NO", it should be enough to stop him from reacting.

The next test is to introduce him to another dog and if you know someone who has a well-balanced dog you can pre-arrange to meet either in the street or park. To begin with, keep him on a longish lead and let him go up to the nice dog and let them sniff each other. If he is a bit full on, pull him away and say "NO" and then allow him to go back and say hello again. Dogs sniff bums and things which are quite natural. If there is a grumble pull him away, chastise, and try again. If you are not happy or confident then you can always put a muzzle on him, meaning the other dog will be quite safe and you can introduce them with more conviction and without any problems.

If you can do this on a daily basis with one dog at a time (do not overdo it) everything will be fine. It is hard work but well worth the effort and if you follow precisely as written, it should only take two weeks to come together. I know it works as I have done it hundreds of times. If you have to ask a total stranger always ask if their dog is friendly, if their response is "Well it can be a bit funny," do not bother. You must have total control over your dog for any of this to be effective.

CASE HISTORY ONE
AGGRESSION TOWARDS OTHER DOGS

People never cease to amaze me when it comes to their dogs, especially when it is such an important problem as aggression. They seem to view it from a totally different perspective from myself, their perspective defies common sense. I have been telephoned a thousand times about aggressive behaviour between dogs, and Mrs Penny was no exception.

"Hello, I have a problem with Harriet, she tries to attack every dog she sees and I have tried everything to stop her but she still insists on going for them and she makes an awful noise when she starts, so something needs to be done," she finished. "Well it can be put right," I said. "What I do is a one to one and I come to you and..." But she interrupted and said, "Oh no, that is no good the dog needs classes it needs to be with other dogs, thanks anyway," and she put the telephone down.

That is a typical phone call about this topic, I don't even get to finish my spiel, good manners prevent me from saying, "I have never heard such rubbish in my life," but I don't get the chance. For those of you who are still in the dark regarding this short conversation, I will explain, as I feel that people really do not understand how it works.

I have explained in Chapter 6 how dogs become aggressive towards other dogs, therefore once this has happened and it is causing problems whilst out walking, it has gone beyond dog training classes and another method has to be put into play. As it turned out Mrs Penny called again two weeks later and never mentioned her initial call so I arranged to go to her house. Having assessed Harriet, I left Mrs Penny to get on with what she needed to do. Effectively Mrs Penny followed Chapter 14, and a fortnight later I arranged to go back. Mrs Penny had followed the instructions to the letter, Harriet did not need a muzzle and we went to the nearest park to await a victim. Harriet was under perfect control and listened to every word Mrs Penny said to her. In the distance we saw another dog approaching, Mrs Penny was well versed in what she had to do and say.

Firstly, we asked the owner of the dog if it was acceptable for us to introduce the two dogs, and if she thought her dog would be alright. The answer was yes, so Mrs Penny, having Harriet on a long lead, let her dog go forward for them to meet. Harriet grumbled with uncertainty, but Mrs Penny pulled her back, said "NO" and let her go forward again. The other dog showed no sign of being afraid. When Harriet went forward again and behaved Mrs Penny praised her and Harriet was encouraged by this and both dogs get on really well. Just to prove to Mrs Penny it was not a fluke, we hung around for another willing victim which was a Jack Russell. We again did the same scenario however this time the Jack Russell was a bit livelier but with careful manipulation of Harriet all went well.

Mrs Penny's reaction was total astonishment, she never envisaged Harriet being friendly with any dog again, but once you know what you are doing it's simples!

CASE HISTORY TWO
AGGRESSION TOWARDS OTHER DOGS

There is another side to dogs that pull on their leads. It is not always to go and fight the other dog as we are too ready to accuse them of. Dogs put on a show when they see a dog coming their way and to the layman it probably looks aggressive, but there are dogs who only want to go and play. Because owners are not sure, they would sooner fear the worst so they stop the dog from its natural ability to interact with its own kind. Again it is down to human failure – by not understanding our best friends as well as we should.

Cats are another reason why a dog would want to pull on its lead, and we would put that down to aggressive behaviour when actually it is a normal situation, a game to most dogs. It is a natural reaction for a dog to chase and what is more exciting for a dog than a cat on the run. Then add wheels (no, not a cat on a skate board!), wheels on a lawn mower, a vacuum cleaner, cyclists, cars, cows, sheep etc. anything on the move will excite a dogs instincts. A dog will chase anything it sees regardless of how many feet or wheels it possesses. It is after all the nature of the beast when looking back at its ancestry; it was the only way it got fed.

All of this can be put to right by the owner taking control. It is not so much as what they are pulling towards, it is the fact that they are allowed to pull on the lead, regardless of what the reasons are. They are a danger to the person who is on the other end of the lead.

Dogs who pull suddenly, without warning, mostly cause damage to their walker. People have been pulled to the ground and sustained broken bones, especially the elderly, and the worst cases are when a dog pulls its walker into the road, under an on-coming vehicle and both are killed. This occurs more often than you realise. Dogs are not human, they have no road sense whatsoever, and just because your dog will sit at the curb it does not necessarily follow that the dog understands why it is sitting there. He is sitting there because he has been told to.

CHAPTER 4
AVERSION METHODS

What is Aversion Therapy or Method? Aversion therapy means using different ways to stop someone doing something you do not want them to do. The exact meaning from a dictionary is "Aversion Therapy", designed to make a subject averse to an existing habit.

Dog training books tells us to use such dog training aids, like nasty smelling sprays, treats, clickers and putting pebbles in a bottle to shake at the dog, the idea is to distract the dog from what it is doing.

Yes, the dog is distracted but only momentarily, you will always need to use these methods, they only mask the problem until you need to use them again the following day. These quick fixes do not cure your existing problem.

These kinds of training methods, in my opinion, are unacceptable. I know they do not work because I have tried them.

As far as your dog is concerned it is only doing what you have inadvertently taught it to do. Meaning, if you had taught your dog correctly in the first place, you would not be using these techniques, which, without doubt, are beginning to fail. By this I mean your pet will be very wary of you. Train your dog correctly and it will be better balanced and will live a happier life.

Bribery is one of the most popular ways to train a dog. They even use bribery at dog training classes. Tell the dog to sit, and then give it a biscuit. Each time you tell the dog to do something for you, it will look to see if you have a treat in your hand before it decides whether to do it or not. It looks good that your dog is obeying your every command, until you run out of treats, or you are out on a walk and your dog is running free and enjoying itself, then it spies something more interesting than its owner, and off it goes and all the biscuits in the world will not bring it back. At least you will have something to eat whilst you are waiting for the dog to return!

Barking is the dog's way of communicating with the world and also to warn us that there is someone or something that is not quite as it should be. So when the dog starts to bark we should be able to step in and take over, but it continues to bark, why? Answer – because it can and it's through our inability to stop it we try all these other methods.

Another habit that our loving pets get up to is stealing, usually from worktops and rubbish bins. The amount of meat joints that have disappeared from worktops is legendary. But these kinds of activities are often not very amusing at the time of the offence. It is not everyone that can afford this type of thing to happen on a regular basis, and trust me, it happens on a regular basis. Waste bins are another favourite of the family pet dog as it leaves half the contents all over the kitchen floor and to add insult to injury, it has eaten the other half of the bin's contents whether they were edible or not.

Nasty, smelly sprays like Bitter Apple or squirts of water seem to be the advice from dog training books, but, like any other quick fix it does not work. You would need to be with your dog all the time to be able to execute these methods.

Thunderstorms and fireworks are commonplace and a complete nightmare for dogs and owners alike at certain times of the year. This again, along with the rest of the problems you will read about here, is another man made problem. Buying gadgets like calming smells to plug in or a CD sounding like a storm to let the dog get used to the sound are all very well but what does the poor dog do while you are out or at work.

As aversion therapies go the electric shock collar is the worst one. In my opinion the collar is a barbaric thing to do to any animal, let alone your family pet dog, but sadly people do use them, always through ignorance and not through the knowledge and understanding of how their pet dog's mind works. The second you put one of these collars on your dog you have not only let yourself down but more importantly you have let your dog down as well. The use of these collars does not cure whatever problem your dog has with another dog, it will only frustrate it and confuse it all the more because it cannot come to terms and conquer its fears or any other issues it might have.

To know how not to get these problems in the first place you will find out in depth in Chapter 1 – Puppies. To find out how to put these problems right you will find in Chapter 11 – Shelter Dogs and Chapter 14 – Discipline.

CASE HISTORY ONE
AVERSION METHODS

I received a telephone call from a very nice man who was having difficulties with his best friend, "Billy", a very friendly staffy.

Mr Bright, the owner of Billy, would spend time most days in the summer, since he was retired, in his front garden with his dog by his side, watching the world go by, reading his books and would pass the time of day with all and sundry who walked past.

Most would bring Billy a tit-bit and Billy loved people and all they had to offer. The only drawback from this idyllic life was other dogs. Each time one passed, Billy would rush to the gate and bark wildly. He did not get on with the dog next door so the two dogs could not be let out at the same time, which caused tension between Mr Bright and his neighbour. Something needed to be done, so I was called in to help. Having listened to what Mr Bright had to say I did mention that taking Billy for a walk must be very difficult. "Oh, no," he said, "I can walk Billy round the lakes without his lead on and he is under control," he said with a smile.

How does that work I thought to myself, he cannot control his dog in his own garden. So I had to ask the question, when I did, Mr Bright stood up and said that he would be back in a second and left the room.

He went out to his car and came back with something I had never seen before. I had heard about them but had not actually seen one in the flesh, so to speak. It was an Electric Shock Collar. As soon as he brought it in and Billy saw it, the dog's demeanour altered immediately, he dropped his head and the friendly happy light in the animal's eyes went out. Then the dog walked away.

I felt so sorry for it I had to say to the owner, if my dog had reacted to seeing the collar as your dog had done, I would be ashamed of myself, at the same time I did have one eye on the door in case I needed to make a hasty retreat. I asked him how many times he actually used the collar, and the answer was every time he took the dog out. "Each time he runs towards another dog, I press the button and it stops him," he said. "The first time I used it I got the voltage wrong and Billy did a back flip," he said with a degree of remorse. "So actually when push comes to shove you do not have any control over your dog, the nasty collar does all the work," I said.

So in short, Billy's instinct to run and have a go at another dog is still there. As I have always maintained, quick fixes do not cure your problem, it just puts it on hold and it will never be put right, the dog will never master the differences it has with its own kind. I explained to Mr Bright all he needed to do to put his problem right. After two weeks I got back in touch with him and his problems were over and Billy was a happier dog and the collar was on Ebay (so do not be silly enough to buy it, I can tell you now that it does not work!).

The second time I encountered this barbaric approach to dog training was when a customer rang me with a problem. Prior to me going out to see him the owner had already had a dog trainer out to help him, but I was not informed about the other trainer until I was leaving.

One of Mr Brownlow's problems was that when he took his dog out in the car it would bark at everything that moved. So when the trainer came he told Mr Brownlow to get into the car and that he would put the dog in the back for him, mumbling something like "Do not worry about him barking I will sort it." Mr Brownlow and his dog, plus trainer, set off. Mr Brownlow was very surprised that his dog was only making muffled noises instead of barking. He was very impressed, how amazing, this man had cured his problem so soon, it had only been ten minutes. It was only when they got back home that the so-called dog trainer showed him what he had done and how good these collars were. Mr Brownlow was devastated and when he told his wife she went ballistic, and as far as I know she is still orbiting the earth.

CASE HISTORY TWO
AVERSION METHODS

I answered the telephone one Boxing Day to a very distraught lady. "Hello," she said in a strained voice. "I have been given your number by someone who said you could help me with my problem, I am sorry to ring you over Christmas but I am desperate," she said. "It is quite alright", I said trying to make her feel at ease and at the same time glad of the distraction and very conscious of my uncle Reg, who was making his usual annual nuisance of himself.

"It is my little Westy, "Freddy", he has just snapped at me and he has caught my hand," she continued. "Freddy has had a go at me before but this time he has bitten me quite badly," she said with an undercurrent of total disbelief in her voice that little Freddy was capable of doing such a nasty deed. "Right," I said, "do not worry; tell me all about it from the beginning."

So to cut a very long story short, Freddy has a habit of rushing towards the front door and grabbing the post when it arrives and then proceeds to rip it to shreds. Freddy's other little vice is to jump on to the furniture and will not get off when told. It is especially annoying when the dog has been out in the rain.

So Mrs Clark, having read somewhere that each time Freddy ignores a command, like leave or get off the furniture, she should squirt him with a jet of water right in the face. This worked the first time simply because he was shocked into getting off the furniture. But the water fell short when he went for the post and it only made matters worse. Freddy started to snap and snarl at his owner.

The dog's sheer determination to rip up the post was more important to him than anything its owner did or said. This show of total disrespect is brought on, like all problems, because the owners are far too soft with their dogs. Until Mrs Clark took proper control over Freddy, without using props and distractions, she was always destined to fail.

We have to remember that Freddy follows an instinct, something that he, like all other dogs, are born with and abide by. It is inherent in them (a word you will read a lot about in this book) and it is a code that we need to invest time and appreciation into cracking. Until we know what makes a dog tick, there will always be a Mrs Clark.

CHAPTER 5
DIAGNOSING PROBLEMS

All dogs display, in one form or another, the way they are feeling, just like we do and it's called body language.

If the dog is happy and pleased it will wag its tail and be very fussy. If it is angry or alert to danger, the hackles will rise at the back of the dog's neck. On the other hand, if the dog has been told off it will put its tail between its legs and slink away to a quiet place and settle down. Either way it will be demonstrating its true feelings.

All these signs we are well aware of and we understand them. There are some signs, especially of dominance, which are a different kind of behaviour, which our pets exhibit that we misread. It is these underlying behavioural problems which we do not understand and it is neglecting these which make our pet dog a danger, not only to us, but to other people. Therefore how do we read our dog better and how do we know when our pet is slowly but surely taking over?

Our dogs have subtle ways of showing dominance. All dominant dogs think that they are important, so everything revolves around them. In their minds they have to make all the decisions and to do this properly they have to keep an eye on the comings and goings of the family, so it can keep everyone in their place.

Some dog's favourite place is lying halfway up the stairs or on a landing so it has the advantage point of looking down on everyone and monitoring their movements. A small dog will use the back of a chair or sofa to look down on everyone and keep a watchful eye for the next person to move.

Another subtle little trick to look out for is when you are busy in the kitchen or you are cooking a meal, the dog will lie in front of appliances or areas which it knows you frequently need to use. It could be the cooker, the fridge or a cupboard. You may ask why the dog would lie there if it continuously has to move. Apart from the constant attention it will receive from you (which dogs thrive on) it also knows that to get to where you want to be you have to pass the dog first. In addition, another preferred place to lie is in doorways or where a room divides. Here again you will have to ask the dog to move out of your way or stride over it to be able to exit the room. This can be difficult depending on your age or if you are carrying an item, such as a tray or child.

Also, there are times when we are watching the television as a family and look around for the dog only to find that it has taken itself off into another room and is in its bed fast asleep. Dogs, as we all know, are like us, they are also pack animals and as such we should all be together. Every pack has a leader and the head of the pack will eat and sleep away from the rest, which is its privilege. Therefore, the dog has detached itself from the rest of the pack and is sleeping alone, just like leaders do.

Another misconception is when a dog wets in the house. A dog will wet in the house for three reasons. One, it is not properly house-trained. Two, it is suffering from what is known as separation anxiety. Three, is through dominance.

To briefly explain these problems. The separation anxiety is both wetting and soiling and is usually done when the dog is left alone, regardless of whether the owner is in bed or out. Similarly, the lack of house-training, it will do both here and there and not go to the door to be let out. The dominant dog will only wet in the house and this is done when the owner is in or out. It will do it right in front of you. The dog will cock its leg and wet on cupboards, the fridge, furniture, tables and sofas, anything. In the dog's mind it does not think that it has done anything wrong, it's just a natural instinct for it to mark its territory. The dog sees itself as the boss of the house so it will over-mark your smell for its own, in the same way a dog will cock its leg over the markings of another dog whilst it is out walking, simply to establish its territory.

Another popular trait of the dominant dog is mouthing. This is when a dog will put its mouth around your wrist or hand and try to hold it there. We naturally pull away and do not give it another thought, telling the dog to "stop it". But whenever it gets the chance it will continue to do it. The intention is not to bite or hurt it is just to let you know that it is in charge of you and to keep you in your place. This sign of dominance is often misdiagnosed as something totally different. Some people seem to think it is a sign of affection and the dog wants to hold their hand.

In view of the fact we do not understand the signs of dominance, we have a tendency to make excuses for the way our dog behaves if it disappears into another room or takes itself off to its bed, we just think that it is cooler in the other room or the dog is tired.

Even when it lies in front of cupboards we think it wants to be near us. Therefore, by not reading the signs correctly we are inadvertently encouraging the dog to rise up the hierarchy ladder.

CASE HISTORY ONE
DIAGNOSING PROBLEMS

Misreading a situation is a very common occurrence with dog owners. It makes life just that little more complicated, especially when they have their mind set on what they think is the problem, and then I go along and spoil their diagnosis by telling them that their dog is taking advantage of their good nature.

One such case came along with a telephone call from a lady. Mr and Mrs Teal had just acquired two Scottie Terriers, which in Mrs Teal's opinion had been badly treated. She knew this because of the way the dogs acted under certain circumstances. For example, when it came to feeding time the owners would put the bowls down and invite them to dine, but instead of rushing forward with appreciation they would stand over the bowls and would not start to eat until the owners had walked away, and then they would fill their boots.

These are just a few of the most popular antics our pets get up to. So if you recognise any of these little traits the answers on how to put them right is found in depth in Chapter 14 – Discipline.

This lead Mrs Teal to believe that the dogs were given a hard time at meal times. If this was the case the dogs would associate feeding times as something to be feared and would not venture anywhere near their feeding bowls.

Another reason why the Teals thought that their dogs had been mistreated was when they were being given a command, something simple like, sit, stay or lie down, the dogs would visibly shake or try and hide somewhere. So Mr and Mrs Teal decided not to pressure the dogs and all the commands stopped.

The other deception the two con merchants came up with (and I do not mean Mr and Mrs Teal), was to convince Mrs Teal that the sofa was a safe haven for them. They would only get off at feeding times, to go to the toilet and when it was time to go for a walk.

These particular problems are not solely down to the Teals, they are problems the two dogs had learnt long before they pitched up at their new abode. Like most rejected dogs they often come with mind boggling baggage. Mrs Teal's main objective was to put her two pets to right and to put them back into society better able to cope with life rather than hiding from it.

When I arrived the husband let me in, and the two dogs were sitting alongside his wife on the sofa, but grumbled when I walked in to the room, giving credence to Mrs Teal's theory. My first job was to ask Mrs Teal if she would tell the dogs to get down from the sofa, which she did without question. The dogs were totally put out and sat looking indignant on the floor. I explained to the owners why their dogs reacted the way they did in certain situations. Why their stood over their bowls waiting for the under dogs (the Teals) to walk away so they could eat in peace. They had learnt somewhere along the way that if they showed signs of discomfort they could get away without doing as they were told, so securing a place on the sofa was a breeze for them.

The chapter on diagnosing problems is about control. It is about how dogs control by dominating their owners. It manipulates situations for their own advantage. Mr and Mrs Teal were well and truly hoodwinked.

CASE HISTORY TWO
DIAGNOSING PROBLEMS

My next case history came from a teacher who had a perfect relationship with her little King Charles Spaniel, "Barney". Wendy had Barney from a pup and they were inseparable, wherever Wendy went Barney would go too. The only time they were separated was when Wendy went to work.

Then suddenly things went pear-shaped. Wendy took a long weekend away and Barney stayed with her parents. When she came back Barney had turned from a loving best friend to quite an aggressive stranger, not only to Wendy, but towards any friends who visited the house.

The dog refused totally to do anything that was asked of it. Each time she tried to tell it to do something it would openly defy her, if she forced the issue it would snap at her and back away growling. If any of her friends came round to the house, Barney would bark and grumble at them, especially when they were leaving. The reaction of her dog led her to believe that when she went away and left Barney he thought she had rejected him and this was his way of retaliating against her leaving him behind. Wendy credited the dog with more sense than it actually has, but then most people do.

Wendy had no idea how she was going to get the original loving relationship back on track; she was at her wits end and thinking of the worse case scenario, and bitterly regretting having left Barney in the first place. In reality it was a disaster waiting to happen.

The whole experience had nothing to do with Wendy going away, that was coincidental.

Barney, without a doubt was spoilt, he was allowed all the perks he really should not have had, and in return he started to control Wendy's life by refusing to do as he was told, and more of what he wanted to do. With his dominant ways he tried to dictate who was allowed in and out of the house.

Wendy followed Chapter 14 and Barney was put to rights in a week. They are back to best of friends but with a few ground rules in place.

CHAPTER 6
OVER-BONDING

What is over-bonding and what does it mean? Over-bonding is when a dog is over attached to its owner/s and cannot cope when left alone. It has been said to me openly, "I don't mind, I think it's cute when they follow me about." Which is a very selfish attitude to take, because at the end of the day both sides are going to mind a great deal.

On the one side there is the blinkered owner who is down hundreds of pounds and more importantly, on the other side is the over devoted dog who is spending time in a 6x4 concrete cell (a slight exaggeration on my part about the size but it is relative all the same), wondering where it all went horribly wrong.

There are several reasons why over-bonding occurs; therefore we will start at the beginning. When we acquire a puppy we tend to spend too much time with the puppy. Time spent with the puppy should be limited, but to be fair problems do happen from being misinformed, either by television, various books, the internet, or Mrs Brown who lives three doors up and who has had dogs all her life and knows what she is talking about!

It does not help the puppy in any way, it only makes it worse. If we were to equate this to children going to school for the first time, nine times out of ten the child will cling to its mother pleading, because it does not want to be left. To a child you can explain that you will be back later to pick them up and until then what a good time they are going to have.

With a dog you cannot explain, you just leave it. When you leave the dog you leave it in a big empty space which it is not accustomed to and it starts to stress. Over-bonding happens at any age, whether it is a puppy or a grown dog, perhaps from a shelter, or even your own dog you have had for some time.

Therefore who makes the dog over-bond? We have discussed the puppy side of it, but it also happens to older dogs. The shelter dog is not always afflicted with this complaint, but it can soon become a problem. Owners tend to over-compensate for the dog's unhappy life and spoil them until they too suffer from it. I have known owners who have had their dog for years and then suddenly the owners find that the dog has over-bonded. This usually occurs if the dog has been ill, off its food, or had a spell being treated by the Vet. It is just like having children, if they are ill we tend to spoil them a little, but with a dog a little spoiling goes a very long way.

Over-bonding shows itself in three ways. One is when the dog is left on its own, it will either mess everywhere, howl and bark the whole time the owner is out, or it will be very destructive. It is rare that a dog will display all three, but it does happen. If your dog fouls in the house occasionally, you only have to leave the room for it to do something, but the last thing to do is to chastise the dog, it already has a problem and you will only make it worse by making it an issue.

When you get up in the morning and the dog has messed, you greet your little friend as if nothing has happened and then put it outside whilst you clean up the mess. You follow the same pattern when you come home.

Two, if your dog is prone to being destructive this is when it costs you more than exasperation, it will chew rugs, wallpaper, books, cds, television remotes, telephones, telephone wiring, cushions, its bed, the list is endless and expensive.

Three, howling is self explanatory, there is nothing you can clear up or put out of harm's way to stop this particular problem, but this on its own creates a problem of a different sort, it is known as irate neighbours.

A dog who is suffering from over-bonding, has, as I have mentioned before, far too much space to panic in, so all we have to do is minimise the amount of space so it has less room to panic in. This is one of the rare moments in which a cage can come in handy. You must remember that you cannot just put the dog in a cage and leave it at that; you have to put the problem right, the dog is very unhappy and is suffering, and no one wants that. If you do not have room for a cage, a small hallway or the kitchen will work just as well.

To resolve this problem follow Chapter 14 – Discipline.

CASE HISTORY ONE
OVER-BONDING

I received a call one day from a Mrs Bradley. "Hello, I have just got a dog, well I have had her two weeks, she is a little Sheltie, called Poppy, and she is two years old. She is very loving and we get on well together. I got her from a shelter. At first things seemed to be OK then the odd accident here and there but nothing major," she said. "But when I came home from work she had chewed the skirting board and pulled the wallpaper from the wall. Just a few things at first and now every time I come home she has destroyed something else. The house is rented and I cannot afford to keep putting things right. I do not want to take her back, you are my last hope."

I went to see Mrs Bradley and looked at Poppy's handiwork, and yes she had made a mess. Therefore, as I have mentioned before, when a dog over bonds it stresses and in a big area it makes it worse, so limiting the space the dog is left in helps it to cope. I know that it is not always possible to have a cage when there is very little room, so we then have to make do with what we have. In Mrs Bradley's case she had a small hallway near the back door. This is where we decided it would be a good area to keep Poppy. There was nothing in there that would be of any danger to her and nothing she could destroy. We closed all the doors leading from the hallway and put Poppy's bed, water and some of her toys in there. It was turned into a snug little place for Poppy to go to at night and when Mrs Bradley was at work.

You can utilise most places, a kitchen, a cupboard under the stairs, or a utility room or a small hallway like Mrs Bradley's. But this little den alone would not benefit Poppy at all if it was just left there. Mrs. Bradley had to put Poppy through her paces; she needed to follow Chapter 14 – Discipline, to the letter. She did exactly that. Poppy now has the run of the ground floor and is a well balanced happy dog.

CASE HISTORY TWO
OVER-BONDING

A Mr York phoned one day with the attitude of a person who had had enough. He worked shifts which complicated things for him. He has had Monty from a puppy and like 65% of owners and their dogs; they were made for each other. It was because Mr York worked shifts that he made up the time by over compensating and so Monty over-bonded and then things went pear shaped.

He would allow Monty into the bedroom to sleep and in between shifts he would always be making a fuss of Monty to make up for leaving him. Then Mr York came home and found that Monty had been fouling in the house. One day a friendly neighbour informed him that Monty was barking and howling whilst he was at work and he was bothered that some of the other neighbours were going to complain.

Mr York thought that Monty was bored and brought him a friend home from a shelter. They got on very well whilst Mr York was there but the barking and howling still continued when he was at work, and the fouling too. To save the house from Monty's fouling and thinking some exercise would be good for them he built a kennel and a run in his garden for the dogs when he was at work. Unfortunately the barking and howling never stopped and because he worked shifts the noise to the neighbours seemed to be constant. Mr York was doing it all wrong and he was never going to get out of the predicament he found himself in.

Eventually someone did call the council to complain. When a complaint is made, the council is duty bound to investigate. If it is found that the barking is an issue they may serve a Noise Abatement Notice. If the notice has been served and the barking does not stop then prosecution is a very real possibility. The council gave Mr York my number and between us we sorted out the problem.

Adding an extra dog to give Monty company was not the way to go, Mr York had misdiagnosed Monty's problem. I know people who have ten dogs and one who had over-bonded – the other dogs did not make it feel any better.

CHAPTER 7
CHILDREN AND DOGS

Dogs and children, what a combination! Wherever you see children there is always a dog tagging along keeping its eye on things whilst the children frolic in the grass, down by the river fishing, having a picnic and generally having fun. The only thing in the sky apart from the sun is the sound of bird song, and so at the end of a very long perfect summer's day, limbs browned by the summer sun and happy little faces, are rounded up like sheep and herded safely home. This is the epitome of tranquillity if you lived in the times when Enid Blyton and Timmy were around, but unfortunately we do not, those days are long gone. In reality it is nothing like the picture I have just painted.

The difference between children and dogs are that they do not speak the same language, and apart from the obvious bits, this is the only difference between the two. As far as educating them goes, if we were to exclude an eight week old puppy and a very young child from everyday life for several months, then we introduce them into society they would have no idea how to behave properly, they would run amok. For over twenty years I have dealt with undisciplined dogs and, as far as the children are concerned, I know this for a fact (I witness it happening in Asda every Saturday).

What is not taught cannot be learnt. There are some things which do not come naturally, for example, teaching a child to read and write and the simple task of tying a shoe lace. Where dogs are concerned – house training, lead walking, recall, the basic sit, stay and down, without these essential elements we have nothing, we have no control. That is what is lacking, we do not have to go to the extreme like excluding, we manage to cause havoc without trying.

Dogs need to be trained to obey rules and regulations and know their place in our pack. Feeding them tit-bits to get the dog to do a simple task is bad practice. If we were scored on training methods this one would be zilch. By using the technique the relationship between owner and dog is tenuous to say the least, and if the fate of our children's well-being relies on such ridiculous training methods then there is little wonder of horrific happenings.

As we know, respect is earned and not bought, if we were to ask our child to clear the table or any other little job, you would not be expected to reward them by payment. You would hope that the task is done from the respect and discipline you have with your child. Therefore, respect between dogs and children is something that has to be worked at if it is to be achieved. On one hand we have a dog who needs discipline from the start, and on the other we have children who need educating about the dangers of dogs – not all dogs are friendly, your own might be to a point, but the next one they come across may not be. Many times I have seen children teasing dogs as they walk past at a gate, or if the dog is on the other side of a fence the children will scream and chase up and down winding the dog up. It is not sensible for children to do this and it must be discouraged.

Dogs are not toys to be carried around, stroked whilst they are asleep, on knees and on furniture and anywhere else which is out of bounds, especially not the child's bedroom. Although children think it is great, the dog sees it from a different perspective. It sees the child as someone to use, to play

and to dominate, and as the child shows no authority, it is seen as an easy target. It is not the bogeyman under the bed the child needs to worry about, it is the one on the bed which needs watching.

If we treat dogs firmly but fairly, they would stay as they have been and follow their own instincts, which is looking after the pack and its territory, that is what they are good at and why we get on so well and the term "man's best friend", was born. Unfortunately we have made a right horlicks of things and now every dog born will not grace us with its amazing qualities, it will be moulded by us into something even we do not recognise.

Introducing your pet dog to a new addition to the family is relatively easy. Firstly, we have a dog we have had a while and we think the world of him. Then we are informed that we are adding a new member to our family, the question you have to ask yourself is, is the family pet up to scratch? Ask yourself a few simple questions, e.g. does he sit immediately when asked to, immediately being the operative word, will he come back when called, stay, and stop barking when told to? If the answers to these questions are NO, then you need to remedy this and reading Chapter 14 will sort out your problems.

To be fair 99% of my calls relating to pregnant mothers and their dogs are for me to go and put the dog right well before the baby is born and everyone lives happily ever after. Then you get the odd one or two who know that their dog is not up to scratch and they do nothing about it until it is too late and then the dog has to go. If your dog is well balanced when the baby arrives, do not alienate him from the baby by shooing him away, let him go up to the baby and have a sniff, let him be there when you feed, change and cuddle baby. We also know that with a baby there are the family, the neighbours and it is not long before the house is full to the rafters with people, here again the dog is just as important and should not be side-lined into another room.

When all the activity has quietened down at the end of a very long day you can have your special moments with your dog. Keep him in the loop and everything will be fine.

CASE HISTORY ONE
CHILDREN AND DOGS

If on a scale of 1-10 and if I was going to get rich on any one dog problem, the most popular one would be grandparents; grandparents spoiling their dog and their grand-children. It's a 10 (but I do not charge enough to get rich!).

Grandparents are famous for letting things slide with their dogs and saying, "We don't have a problem with the dog." You would be surprised at the amount of stuff (a technical term) that people will put up with concerning their dog's behaviour. Half of them will say "it's alright I can cope." With the emphasis on I, and the other half think it is normal behaviour and get on with it.

The conversation starts in the usual way, "Hi, our dog, Brodie, is a loving little thing but he can be nasty, he will try it on with me and my wife Edith, given half a chance. I'm Reg, by the way, but it's the grandchildren who bother me, he has started to grumble at them."

To cut a very long story short the gist of it is, that when the grandchildren go round Brodie is very pleased to see them and runs towards them showing nothing but excitement at their visit. Outside they go, the two children and the dog playing footie. Then in they would come after playing. If Brodie was resting and the children went near to stroke him, his tail would wag and he would enjoy their attention. If they approached him an hour later, if Brodie was not asleep, he would growl. The same thing happened whilst the dog was eating, one minute the children could walk past him and then on another occasion he would growl at them.

In Reg's own words, "The dog grumbled at us sometimes but has never bitten us, we are not bothered about ourselves, it is the children we worry about." So they started to put Jekyll and Hyde into another room whenever the children came round, needless to say the relationship between dog and grandchildren hit rock bottom because the dog was showing its authority over lesser mortals than itself. The children were showing Brodie far too much attention, ignoring him now and again would have been more productive.

Reg and Edith put their collective foot down and now everyone is happy again.

CASE HISTORY TWO
CHILDREN AND DOGS

I was stopped in the street one day by a very upset grandmother. She told me that her daughter and her husband had a Lhasa Apso and his name was Toby. The couple had had Toby from a puppy and absolutely doted on him, he went everywhere with them, he even slept with them, discipline was not evident at all and at times. Elsie (the grandmother), would look after Toby whilst the couple went away on holiday, or away at weekends. Toby, in her opinion, was spoilt and would not obey commands. He would growl if you tried to enforce a command and no one was allowed near him when he was eating. All these things were not just aimed at her and her husband; he would react in the same way towards Linda and her husband, who are Toby's owners.

"I keep telling her to do something about it," said Elsie, "because it is getting out of hand, he will not even get off the chair if you want to sit down and in fact he openly dares you to get him off." All this sounded familiar, and I thought I knew where this was going until she informed me that her daughter was pregnant with twins and Linda and her husband, Terry, could not risk keeping him, so they are going get rid of Toby. In a perverse kind of way she seemed upset more about Toby going. "Oh, don't get me wrong," she said, reading my facial expression correctly, "there must be a way of putting this whole mess right, Toby has been part of their family and should remain so, I was hoping if Toby could be put right they would not have to let him go."

I told her there was something that could be done, but they had to follow my instructions to the letter. "Oh, they will, I will make sure they do, the trouble is they have never had a dog before and to be fair they really did not have a clue and I think they thought they were doing the right thing."

I visited the couple who were grateful, but according to them they could not see any way round the problem. All the advice they had been given from other people and from the Internet never worked. Although getting rid of Toby seemed to be an easy option I do not think it would have been that simple for them. What makes it worse for them is that they would have given Toby up, and then they would have found out too late that there was help out there after all.

Toby was saved in the nick of time, thanks to grandma.

CHAPTER 8

MYTHS AND OLD WIVES TALES

When I was young (and I am no spring chicken now) I can remember being told that the way to house-train a puppy is, when it messes in the house, you get it by the scruff of its neck and rub its nose in the mess it has just made, then put the dog outside, thereby learning that messing inside the house is wrong.

As we know, going to the toilet is a natural bodily function, whether we like it or not it is something which we have no control over, therefore trying to stop a dog, especially a puppy, from messing is virtually impossible. Misleading the dog in this way only confuses and above all, distresses the dog, which adds to your problems.

You would have thought that, after all these years, people would have learned by now that this unseemly conduct does not work, but people I visit are still using this outmoded technique and needless to say, they are struggling. Although they will say to me that the dog knows it has done wrong because when I walk into the room it cowers, my first thoughts are – poor dog, not poor owner. This is down to body language. The only thing that the dog understands is your facial expressions and your tone of voice, so when you walk into the room and find that the dog has messed, your demeanour alters and it is that which the dog is reacting to, it knows what is coming next!

To know how to house-train your puppy you will find in Chapter 1. For an adult dog you will find how to do this in Chapter 11 – Shelter Dogs.

Another myth which is still in practice today is; one dog, one master. In the beginning the dog was usually kept outside on a chain and fed on scraps from the table (if it was lucky). Then the dog got a fortunate break and was allowed inside the house and it was down to the man of the house to train it. This was achieved via a size ten boot, but I am happy to say that some of us have moved on.

Dogs do need to know their place in the great scheme of things and there is no point in one person being able to train the dog. When I visit people in their homes the wife will say to me, my husband trains the dog, I can't do a thing with it. I ask it to do something and it just ignores me. Generally what happens is the wife will ask the dog to "sit" and she may have to ask it more than once, then the husband will say "sit" (usually when the husband says "sit", everybody sits, including the dog). By doing this he has taken over and he has seen the command through what the wife has started. The dog will view her as the weak link because she did not complete the command. That is not good enough; whoever gives the command should see it through; a four year old should be able to put the dog in its place. This way the dog respects all members of the family.

One of the most devastating problems the owner has to face is when they arrive home to find that their furry bundle of fun has run amok and annihilated their home, the furniture is chewed and there is mess and mayhem everywhere. The owners first thoughts are, why? After everything we have done for the dog it has repaid us by doing this. After giving the dog a good telling off, which has gone straight over its head, they clean up.

Some people think behind the dog's behaviour is spite, it did it to spite them, which on the face of it, looks quite feasible, or they will blame boredom, and the dog got bored whilst they were out. Neither of these two answers is correct. Dogs do not do spite or boredom, these are human traits. The destruction is done through anxiety. A well balanced dog when left will generally sleep the whole time you are out and greet you with fervour when you return. To learn how to put this anxiety problem right, you will find in depth in Chapter 11 – Shelter Dogs.

Next in a long line of myths is the misconception regarding Labradors and other breeds which do not deserve their unsolicited title. Labradors are a very popular breed of dog and when you have a popular dog you also get a very popular conception of that breed. According to the owners the trouble with this breed is they cannot stop them chewing, so they ignore the problem and carry on regardless. Labradors do not have the monopoly on chewing (any dog will chew for whatever reason). Subsequently the Labrador goes down in history to the next generation as a breed of dog that chews.

The same mistake is made about Terriers, they nip, and all German Shepherd dogs have a nasty streak along with Staffies. They are all killers.

Inaccuracies are also made about a dog's intelligence. Some of my clients say that their mongrel is thick and slow to understand, and then on the other hand someone will have a pure bred and still complain about their ability to retain a command, although they will say it is willing to learn. All dogs are born equal, by this I mean they, like us, have the ability to learn. It is how we get the message across to the dog that fails both parties. If we get it wrong the dog will get it wrong. Until people are educated about these fallacies undeserving legacies will live on.

AGGRESSION TOWARDS FAMILY MEMBERS AND VISITORS

Aggression towards family members from their fun loving pet dog is very common. 80% of dogs have, at one time or another, either grumbled, growled or have even bitten their owners, their children, and in many cases, visitors to their homes.

The question is, why? Why do dogs turn suddenly from being a happy chappie to an intense over protective teeth bearing fiend! The answer to that is, they don't. Most aggression evolves, it happens over weeks and sometimes it can be months before it actually rears its ugly head.

Aggression is a symptom, not an actual condition. It is built up from several other problems that are distinguishable from the norm, but they are only distinguishable from the norm if you know what you are looking for.

Some people believe that dogs are born with a nasty streak. This is not so, unless of course they are born with a mental defect. Aggression is taught, it is our defect in how we train them that is the problem.

To understand the symptoms before they get out of hand, check out Chapter 5 – Diagnosing Problems. This chapter will inform you on what to look for.

Spoiling our dogs is the main cause of our problems, although spoiling is a subjective word. What spoiling means to one person does not necessarily mean the same to another. (I thought I would explain for the younger reader to save you from referring to the dictionary!) But the end result is still the same.

We give our dogs far too much leeway, perhaps more than we would our children. (Either way they are both capable of biting back!). Something as simple as giving the dog a bed to sleep on. It will immediately perceive this as its own, so much so that they growl and grumble at anyone who should wander by a little too close to its bed on which it happens to be lording over. Some people refer to the dog's bed as its own space and it should be allowed to be left in peace on it.

The dog should not have its own space, only the top dog is allowed that perk. If you must give your dog a bed put it down at bedtime and when you go out. Along with their own beds we also give them the freedom of curling up on our sofas, chairs and then to top it all we allow them on our beds at night. When you consider how they used to live out in the wilds, they did not pull out a sofa at bedtime and then all pile on to it.

Dogs treat toys very much with the same attitude. We give them toys to play with and why not, dogs love to play, as we do, but there again they get possessive with them and grumble when we go near them. Once the dog has started to be aggressive towards what it sees as its possession, and that includes people, it will become second nature and it will need to maintain its status of which it has become accustomed.

This kind of behaviour we have initiated by believing that our pet dog is an extension of our family, so much so, that we treat them as equals. You may laugh but there are some people who actually give this outrageous notion credence. Nature dictates, because of the dog's deep rooted undomesticated ancestry, it is never going to be possible.

We must look upon the education of a dog like a creative work of art, to produce what is socially accepted is a dog that is under our control and a credit to us. We should put into society what we expect to take from it, and at the end of the day who wants to be governed by a dog! This last statement is not as far off Mars as you might think. Some people are controlled by their dog. In some homes the dog decides who moves and who does not around the house. Because it cannot actually stop them, it will growl and bark at them. If you have heard the old adage, the dog will let you in but will not let you out, is perfectly true.

Although a dog, and this depends on its size, cannot physically stop you from entering the house it will have a good try, but once the door is opened and you are allowed in by the owner, the dog will reluctantly have to accept this. Some dogs will charge at the visitor solely to intimidate them, some will charge and are known to bite the unsuspecting person to keep them at bay. Therefore when it is time to leave, the dog will escort the visitor to the door, with some dogs snapping at their heels.

CASE HISTORY ONE
AGGRESSION TOWARDS FAMILY MEMBERS AND VISITORS

It was an upset customer who called one evening and asked for my help. He asked me if I could call round to his house and help him and his dog, Benny, who was a Straffordshire Terrier.

The customer, Mr Hopkins, told me that he and his dog are in a whole load of trouble (his words) and could not see how he and his dog were going to emerge from this together, it was, as Mr Hopkins put it, the worst case scenario.

He told me that Benny was very obsessive with his toys and his bed; he would not allow anyone near them. One day the Hopkins' and Benny were at a village football match. Benny had with him a stick which was on the ground in front of him, when a nine year old boy wandered up and, seeing the stick and the dog, bent down to pick up the stick. It was whilst the boy was bending down that Benny jumped forward and bit the boy on the face.

It was at this point that all hell broke loose. Most were baying for the dog's blood and verbally abusing the Hopkins' for owning a dangerous and uncontrolled dog. Under such bombardment Mr Hopkins knee-jerk reaction was to set about punishing his dog, it was the last thing he wanted to do, but under the circumstances he was damned if he did and damned if he didn't.

So to cut to the chase, Mr Hopkins was, at the end of the day, summoned to Court to face charges of owning a dangerous dog, which automatically put Benny on death row, and to top it off, Mr Hopkins was reported to the RSPCA for cruelty. To pursue a case of cruelty like this it has to be proved to have been a constant act of cruelty, to have a lasting effect on the dog for it to have reacted the way it did to the nine year old boy, or anyone else for that matter.

Cruelty was not the reason why the dog had bitten the boy; the answer was much simpler than that. Benny was spoilt and did not want to share his toys or his bed (if you were inclined to want to sleep on it!) When I went to visit Mr Hopkins for the first time, his wife let me in and apologised for her husband who was not at home, he was on his way from work but had been delayed and would be there shortly.

This was actually a perfect opportunity to observe the dog and how it would react to his owner when he arrived home. Benny greeted his owner as if he had been away a week. After the initial greeting Benny was quite relaxed in their company. Mr. Hopkins could raise his voice, arms and make sudden movements and Benny never flinched. He showed no signs of keeping his distance from his owner or even attempting to slink off somewhere to hide. He certainly did not show any signs of constant abuse.

I gave the Hopkins' the recipe which would eradicate all their existing problems and turn Benny into a well balanced, loving, caring dog. I informed them I would return in two weeks to see the finished product.

When I returned two weeks later, Benny was a totally different dog. He was sharing biscuits with Mr. Hopkins' four year old niece and playing fetch with a ball. She would throw the ball and Benny would obediently bring it back for her to throw again, then the little girl picked up the ball and walked away with it.

As for the dog's bed, it was turned into a treat and not a right, put down only twice a day, when they went out and when they went to bed.

After my intervention on the day of the Court case, Benny and his owner were exonerated from any changes against them and they now all live happily ever after.

CASE HISTORY TWO
AGGRESSION TOWARDS FAMILY MEMBERS AND VISITORS

Mrs Watson left me a message on my answering machine, she sounded very unhappy, so when I called her back she was almost in tears. "My dog, Jack," she said, "is a Maltese and has bitten my neighbour, she only came round to deliver a parcel, I asked her in and Jack ran towards her and then bit her on the leg." She paused for breath, "I'm mortified, I cannot believe it," she said near to hysteria, "I know Jack has been very bossy lately and very protective of us all, but this

is right out of character, he has never done this before, I don't want to have to put him down, we love him too much, it would break our hearts, is there anything you can do?" she said pleadingly.

I visited Mrs Watson and met her husband and their 4 children. I requested that they kept Jack in another room until I was ensconced with the rest of the family in the sitting room. When we were ready Jack was allowed in. He entered the room breaking the speed limit, he ran straight up to the stranger in the camp, barking and growling in a very aggressive manner. When he eventually stopped he settled down and kept his counsel in the middle of the room, he was quite happy providing no one stepped out of line.

Because I have encountered this problem many times I knew exactly what was going to happen. One of the children stood up to leave the room and the dog immediately leapt up and attacked the feet of the boy and started to bark furiously and spun in circles in a total frenzy, brought on by pure frustration.

The whole family thought it was hilarious that the dog had performed his party piece and they would encourage it whenever they could, unaware of the stress they were causing Jack each time they did it. This display of aggression dictates that it is only a matter of time before someone gets seriously hurt as Mrs Watson's neighbour found to her cost, a bigger dog would have caused more damage.

What is actually happening here is we have given the dog the job of running the house, keeping its eye on people, where they go and what they do. Once the dog has mastered the people indoors it then tries to master the people outside who are trying to get in.

CHAPTER 10
ADOLESCENT DOGS

The adolescent dog, through no fault of its own, finds itself in deep trouble; it is either put to sleep or left at a shelter. This is the age of a dog, when a client phones me; I know it is going to be trouble. Half of the complaints involve the police one way or another. It is mostly, but not always, about biting people, sheep chasing, frightening people and children in the park, chasing horses – every anti-social behaviour you can bring to mind. An adolescent dog, if not controlled, will be doing all of these things and more. The best bit is that the owners have no idea; they see little traits and think it is all part of growing up until someone comes hammering on the door complaining loudly.

It is the most dangerous age, by the time a dog is eighteen months old it should have had its fair share of discipline, if not, then they are a disaster waiting to happen.

Eight weeks old is a good age to start, the dog needs to be nurtured and shaped into what a dog should be and we should take its attributes and make it work for us.

Therefore start at the beginning – we have invited a bundle of fun into our world and then we vow to look after and protect him for all of its life, but although we have good intentions we really must take time to understand the enormity of what we are taking on. Ask yourself these simple questions. Is it a bird and do birds kill? – answer no. Is it a rabbit and do rabbits kill? – answer no. Is it a dog and do dogs kill – answer yes. It might sound over the top but it is true.

The unchallenged young pretender believes that all humans are beneath them and all family members are to toe-the-line. They are there only for the constant needs and attention of the dog, in short, there is no one person in the pack which is above the dog's status.

This kind of dog will grumble if pushed too far, it will not follow commands readily unless there is something in it for itself. He will occupy all the major areas in the house nearest to the fire, the best place on the sofa, moving everybody else off, and on the owner's bed, pushing the husband out, providing he gets in at all. These dogs do not play properly when you play ball, for example, the dog never brings the ball back, he always wants to play on his terms, if you get him to play at all. Although this could be said about most dogs, to the trained eye there is a subtle difference.

Some dogs can be quite forceful in the way they react, especially when friends or family who live away come to stay. The dog will treat them as if they have no right to be there, as far as the dog is concerned it is his house and the visitors are not welcome. Visitors may find it hard to move about the house without being intimidated and when they start to leave, the dog has something to say about that as well, it will run at them barking quite savagely and at times will bite.

The epitome of a high ranking dominant dog is its position in the house. It is paramount that he stays on top by using every trick in the book. He will soon find the weakest link and if the owners are too soft and it goes unchecked, this adolescent dog can be very dangerous. Even an eight week old puppy will want to rule the world.

The owners of such a wayward dog either do not know or do not care much about discipline. This statement is not directed to any particular section of society; it can be true of anyone. People think they are doing a good job giving their dog lots of love and affection and far too much freedom, without them even having to work for their privileges and when disaster strikes, the owners never see it coming. It is always a surprise when their loving little bundle of fun dashes out into the street and bites some poor unsuspecting passer-by, then the owners are mortified, yet the dog acts like a thug in the house and they expect it to act like an angel when it is out and about.

It is a criminal offence if your dog bites someone, it will be deemed as dangerous and out of control. These dogs don't only bite they can kill too.

All is not lost, Chapter 14, is well worth a read and you could save not only your dog's life but a child's life too.

CASE HISTORY ONE
ADOLESCENT DOG

The phone rang one day and a gentleman spoke, "Hello there, is that the behaviourist?"

"Yes," I replied.

"My name is Mr Good and I have two Collies, one is two years old and he is from a rescue centre, the other is nine months old and we have had him from fourteen weeks old. Bobby the older dog is very keen and yesterday he ran into the street and bit a woman on the leg as she was passing. Consequently, the police have visited and we need help."

I made arrangements to meet Mr and Mrs Good at their house. When I arrived both dogs were in the garden simply because the Good's wanted the dogs out of the house whilst I settled in the sitting room awaiting the onslaught. The garden was like a battlefield. The dogs had dug deep holes in the beautiful lawn everywhere you looked. It was obvious at first sight that these dogs spent far too much time outside. I learnt later that the temporary fencing surrounding certain areas of the vast garden was to keep the dogs off parts of it so it could recuperate, and looking at it, discipline was none existent.

I was told that they were both very active dogs, but Bobby was the most wayward, he would run along the side of the fence every time the neighbour was out. The neighbour was so put out about the dog's aggressive manner as it ran along the fence that he complained to Mr Good, so he put another fence temporarily to keep the dog away from the original one. All this messing about simply because Mr Good could not control his dog. Bobby was so out of control that it frightened the neighbour so much so he had to complain. You can imagine the extent of the dog's menacing behaviour as the original fence was 7ft high.

Once Bobby had clocked me, he ran to the French windows with murder in his eyes (slight exaggeration), he certainly did not want to lick me. They were brought in on leads, Ben the younger one, just ignored me, it could not care less. Bobby was totally different, he was more intense and he was very threatening, after all I was sitting in his house without his permission, but he had to be muzzled as it was the only way the two of us could stay in the same room together.

I explained what Mr and Mrs Good had to do to put this problem right so we put the two dogs through their paces. When the dogs were walking around, Bobby came up to me several times his tail wagging but I knew what he was thinking. As for Ben, he never bothered about me, never even came to say hello. He paid no attention to me whatsoever; he is another one for the psychologist's couch but in a totally different way to Bobby.

I learnt after the conclusion that the Good's have only been cautioned and seeking expert help and advice to put their dog right was not on the police agenda. According to the law it is a criminal offence if your dog bites anyone. Are the authorities doing enough to ensure that people are safe to walk down the street or anywhere else without being attacked by some person's out of control dog? If the authorities are only going to do half the job what is the point. The owners of dogs who bite could not get it right first time round so unless they do something about their dog it will almost certainly happen again. Will it be at the cost of someone else, is a child going to be bitten, attacked or killed? In my opinion getting expert advice should be a condition of the caution or do they want every dog in Britain wearing a muzzle. It is not everyone who has a social conscience like the Good's.

When I left Mr. and Mrs. Good's house, Bobby ran at me and he was making some very vicious noises even though he was muzzled he managed to have the last word.

CASE HISTORY TWO
ADOLESCENT DOG

Here is another story of a Collie out of control, only because the owners, as with most owners, have got the wrong idea of what a dog is and what is expected of us on how we should treat the dog. People tend to think that because it is a Collie above all else it must be exercised constantly, and they seem to spend all their spare time walking and entertaining the dog and not enough time is spent on discipline. Any breed of dog will have our attention 24-7 if we allow this.

Yes, we do have dogs which are specifically bred for certain activities, but all these dogs bred for different abilities have to be under strict control. If you can just imagine what it would be like if all the herding dogs were let loose on their own, the Collies and the like would be rounding up the farmers, sheep and cattle, the same with the rat catching dogs, gun dogs, they are all good at what they do, but behind every working dog there is an experienced owner, and it is they who have the control. This is not to say that anyone cannot own a dog which is capable of doing a job, in fact most of us do, but some people have the wrong idea about the dog's needs. It does not need to be doing something all of the time, this was the near downfall of Frank and Linda Turner.

This is a story about a couple who had brought a Collie from a puppy and doted on him, and when he became too boisterous they did not know what to do. Linda was frightened of him, because Frank had taken him on, and he followed Frank everywhere, and Linda had no dealing with the dog at all. Frank had to be away from home for a few nights and Linda had to look after him, but Murphy wasn't having any of it, Linda was scared of putting her foot down and the dog took advantage of this.

It came down to "Either the dog goes or I do." Therefore they sent Murphy away for three weeks to be trained. At the end of the three weeks they went to bring him home. The trainer had him on a lead and as soon as Murphy recognised his owners he pulled towards them, the trainer hit Murphy with a stick to stop him pulling. This was so distressing for Frank and Linda, especially when they realised how Murphy must have been trained...

Once home, Murphy was quiet and meek for couple of days and then reverted to type. This is where I come in. When Frank phoned me he was at his wits end, Murphy was totally out of control. He would not obey under any circumstances; it was as if he was punishing his owners for sending him away (he wasn't of course).

When I arrived, Frank had to bring Murphy in on a lead and he barked and barked in my face, never growled or grumbled, just barked. We put him through his paces and tried, in the time I was there, for Linda to get some control; I had to stop him focusing only on Frank. Linda was a little timid in the beginning but she soon got the hang of it and before I left Murphy was off his lead and sniffing me calmly, and Linda was growing in confidence. This was only the first few steps, once I had departed that would be when the hard work would start. With help and guidance they were now going in the right direction. At the end of the day what brought them through this was that they both loved the dog and they understood that Murphy's problems were brought on by their lack of understanding.

CHAPTER 11
SHELTER DOGS

I always want to applaud people when they get a dog from a shelter and I am always amazed at the number of people who actually do this. I know what an undisciplined dog is capable of doing and I do not want this to sound like a backhanded compliment, but there are people out there with more love in their hearts than sense. Most of these undisciplined dogs come from either shelters or a well meaning person who cannot cope any longer and gives the dog away to a friend or relative or even advertise it in a newspaper.

I know what damage a shelter dog can do and I am quite capable of dealing with them. I would always go for a pup because I can put my stamp on it from the beginning as this is the most important time in a young animal's life. When we get a puppy from eight weeks old we know exactly what we are getting. You start with a clean slate and the only mark on that slate is what nature has provided. Then it is the turn of nurture to provide and that is down to us. If what we put in is put there correctly then what comes out is acceptable.

When we get a dog from a shelter we do not have a clue what we are getting. Dogs are put into these places for numerous reasons and this last recession did not help. The number of pets and this includes cats, which were put into shelters was a very depressing number.

Before we get a dog from a shelter there are things we need to know and understand before we take it home with us. It is typical that when we go to these places the kids just look at them and say, "Ooh Mum, Dad, I want that one it looks so cute and so sad." They all look like butter wouldn't melt, that is their undercover demeanour, dogs in shelters are more undercover than Ethan Hawk (and he's good!).

Most dogs that go into these places have gone in because they have problems, brought on by owners who do not appreciate the workings of a dog's mind. Each dog that goes in, goes in on pretences, and these are usually false ones. Their owners will disguise the real problems by giving made up reasons for why their pet is there. For example, they are moving into rented accommodation and cannot take their pets or moving abroad. The excuses are endless and the truth is not revealed until you get the dog home.

When you go to get a dog from a shelter there are rules and regulations to taking them home which we have to adhere to in order to get the dog, but there are some rules that are over the top. There are two big issues I have with some shelters. One big failing is that they do not let dogs go to people who go to work. Dogs are very adaptable and will live quite happily around peoples' working life if executed properly. My dog does – you ask him where he would rather be. My second bugbear is that we have to give a dog at least two weeks to settle in before we start training it. There is little wonder that the shelters are bulging at the seams, because these stipulations are unnecessary. That is my professional opinion.

Now that we have negotiated the red tape and we have actually got the dog home, if we were to follow the shelter's advice and wait until the dog has got its paws well and truly under the table, you would find within two weeks (or before in some cases) the dog will show its true colours and the real reason why it was in the shelter. This is where the shelter's advice goes horribly wrong. Once this has happened it is very difficult to stop,

especially if you do not know how to put it right. We need to remember the dog's basic instinct, and that it is here to produce and protect the pack and its territory, not so far off what we do.

They are an early warning system to let everyone know that there is someone or something about that should not be there. They should bark to deter the alleged intruder until someone in authority from the pack comes to see what all the fuss is about. The day you get your new friend home you should have decided beforehand where the boundaries lie and the minute it walks through the door those conditions should be put into place. For this you need to follow the advice given in Chapter 14 – Discipline.

With most rescue dogs there will be underlying problems which will need to be addressed as soon as possible. Over compensating is a knee jerk reaction to getting a dog under these circumstances because of its unhappy life, but it will enjoy and feed on your good will and the constant attention we are prone to lavish on our new member of the family. The feedback will not be as complimentary.

Do not let the children crowd around the dog or to start telling it what to do, and definitely not to start cuddling it. This goes without saying but I will say it anyway, never leave a child alone with a new dog. Dominant dogs do not take kindly to being pushed around by what they see as low ranking beings, and children are an easy target for a dog such as this. Therefore, children should take a step back until the parents have had time to put the basic training into place. You do not want to learn this the hard way so following Chapter 14 – Discipline, is vital.

A dog that has been in a shelter will not fare well with other dogs, it is like being in prison, there are dogs that have minor problems and there will be others with major problems, meaning there will be bullies and there will be victims. Here again you will only find out the true facts when you get the dog home. When you get home there will be a few things that will start occurring even whilst you are following the Discipline.

The most likely problems you will encounter will be the dog trying to escape from your property. Some will dash pass you when you open a gate or your front door, or when you take the dog for a walk and let it off the lead. Naturally you do not let the dog run free until you have it under better control. You will learn these things instinctively. How the training is going in the home will be an indication when you start to give the dog the benefit of the doubt outside.

Another popular problem is, when you let your pet out into the garden and then you call it in, the dog just ignores you. Some people assume that the dog has had a very unhappy life indoors and so they make allowance for it and leave it outside so it can come in when it is ready. What is actually happening here is the dog does not want to come in when told; it will come in when it is ready. Freedom is outside and discipline is inside. Another annoying activity you may encounter is quite the opposite from the one above. The dog wants to go outside for a wee, so you get up and let it out, two seconds later it wants to come back in without going to the toilet. Seconds later it wants to go out again and so on and so on until you eventually get its drift and realise that it is only attention seeking. What you need to do in this situation, is to monitor the last time the dog went outside for a wee and a whatsit and not to let it out again for the next couple of hours or so. The next time it tries to convince you that it wants to go out you will know exactly where it is coming from and act accordingly. Dogs acting like this are exerting their control over their new owners just as they used to do with their previous owners.

Over-bonding is a major issue with rescue dogs. We tend to feel sorry for them so subsequently we are too soft with them and that is when they over-bond. Chapter 6 – Over-bonding will correct this.

Not all rescue dogs are house trained. Obviously this depends on how the dog has been brought up. Some owners either do not know or they have been given the wrong information on house training. To cure all your house training problems go to Chapter 1 – Puppies, the cure is still the same regardless of the age of the dog. Adult dogs should be house trained in a week, if they are not then you are doing something wrong! When cleaning up a mess made by an adult dog do not clean the area with a cleaner that contains ammonia, this will only attract the dog back to the same spot.

There is one thing we must remember, that when we come down in the morning to find that the dog has messed, do not tell it off, just put the dog outside and clean up the mess. People will say to me when they are faced with this situation that when they come down in a morning the dog knows exactly what it has done because it will lower its head or slink away into its bed. The dog understands two things from you; one is your tone of voice and your facial expressions. It is your body language that the dog reads; it knows that you are not happy the second you walk into the room. This kind of misunderstanding can lead to a very unhappy dog.

A client of mine had the same problem. She had a German Shepherd bitch who slept in the utility room and every morning when she went in to the dog it had messed and she told it off. Eventually one morning she went into the utility room to find the dog sitting in its basket facing the wall with its back towards the door. It was at this point the owner knew she was doing something radically wrong and needed help. Although the dog had suffered mentally, they are now back on track and best friends again. Therefore, even when the dog reacts it does not necessarily mean that it understands what it has done wrong.

The next big issue people have with their rescue dog is the fear of thunderstorms and fireworks. How this problem develops is quite simple and not complicated at all. It is brought on as usual by an over protective owner with a misguided attempt to protect the dog from a fear it did not know it had. Something similar to parents passing down to their children that they are afraid of spiders or mice, they will, by example, pass on this irrational fear and so the legacy goes on. The main question is how to stop it. If you have gone out and got a puppy from a shelter just follow Chapter 1 – Puppies, to the letter and your pup will never experience this. If it is an older dog you probably will not know until you have a thunderstorm or fireworks. Follow Chapter 14 – Discipline immediately you get the dog home and hopefully you will never find out.

PROBLEM DOG | 69

DEAF DOGS FROM SHELTERS

Deaf dogs can give us just as much love and affection as a hearing dog. When we get a deaf dog from a shelter its ambitions are no different from the ordinary hearing dog. It will still suffer from the usual doggy problems, its wants and needs are still the same and so are the rewards. The only difference between them is that we will have to tackle their problems in a slightly different way.

Once you know what you are doing and get to grips with it, it is just as easy as training a hearing dog. It is the same as communicating with deaf people, use a sign language that both you and your dog can understand and you cannot go wrong. You need to be succinct in your movements and most of all be consistent. Every family member has to use the same body and hand movements.

If you follow the instructions for a normal hearing dog the outcome will be the same. You have to let the dog know its boundaries and what is and what is not acceptable. Training a dog is not totally about what you say, it is the consistency of what you do that makes the difference. For example; you ask a dog to get on to its bed, but the dog just stands there looking at you and ignores your command, what do you do. You have two choices – one you can walk away and leave it, but the moment you do, you have not only lost your authority but you have also lost the dog's respect. Use the second choice if your instructions have failed, because you cannot get the dog onto its bed by using verbal commands you have to get physical. Hold the dog by its collar and put it on its bed, whether the dog is deaf or not, either way you have just completed your request. Then you give the appropriate sign for the dog to sit and stay. Chapter 14 – Discipline, will have more information on this problem.

Deaf dogs need our love, affection and our protection. They come into this world with a defect that is through no fault of their own and the most that we can do is to embrace them and nurture them and turn their lonely misunderstood life around.

CASE HISTORY ONE
SHELTER DOGS

I was asked to visit the proud owners of a Jack Russell called, Troop that Mr and Mrs Naylor had acquired from a shelter, which was promoting itself along with local veterinarian on regional television, informing the public of all the dogs they had in their shelter and the various things the local vet had done for them and now they needed re-homing. This particular dog stole the hearts of many viewers. The new owners were thrilled to bits, not only because the dog was on television but it needed a good home and the Naylors were convinced that they could provide everything the little chap needed.

The Naylors were well informed on what the dog was like and well advised on what they had to do (or so they thought!).

When Mr Naylor rang me he said that the people at the shelter were concerned that the dog had a tendency to have a go at other dogs whilst out walking. Although it walked well on a lead every time it met another dog it would have a go at it. It was this problem that Mr Naylor rang me to rectify, although he had tried various ways of getting this problem right he was getting nowhere fast (his words).

When I arrived at the Naylor house I was invited in and I was quite surprised at the reaction I received from Troop. It was aggressive towards visitors. The information given from the shelter stated it was only aggressive towards other dogs. I was not nervous but very aware that something was not quite right with the dog's attitude. When I mentioned the greeting to the owner he told me he was also concerned about the nastiness that Troop projected not only to visitors but to family members also, and was particularly concerned about his ten year old son.

A dog never just has one problem, it usually has several that lead up to the one big problem that you are concerned about. Get the small ones sorted out and the rest just drop into place. Where children are concerned the sooner it is sorted the better. To do what I needed to do to put things right, I did not want to expose people, especially children, to the training of a dog who has an aggressive attitude. So for this little individual we needed a muzzle. Mr. Naylor said he would buy one and I would return the following day.

At this point, I must repeat and insist that training is done by psychological methods only.

(No dog was harmed during the writing of this book!).

Although this might seem over the top we have to be very careful of dogs we get from other sources, unless of course it is a puppy. Each dog we rescue, regardless of where, it should be put through its paces the minute we get it home.

The following day Mr Naylor phoned me and said he had taken the dog back to the shelter because it had attacked his son who was only sitting on the floor next to his dad. The dog, unprovoked, went for him and had bitten him on the face. To be fair to the Naylors and Troop they only did what they thought was the right thing to do.

For their defence they were only following the instructions given from the shelter and as for Troop he was only following through what he had learnt to do from his previous owners. He was already pre-wired to repeat this wherever he went, which in the end was a devastating lack of discipline and understanding. These things build and take time before they come to the surface.

Whatever happened to the little celebrity is anyone's guess. Dogs are, and I will never tire of saying this, what we make them.

CASE HISTORY TWO
SHELTER DOGS

"Hello, is that the behaviourist?"

"Yes." I said.

"My name is Harry Cliffe and I have a problem with my dog, Ben, and I think you may laugh when I tell you what the problem is", he said. Unless the dog had donned a hat and done the soft shoe shuffle across the kitchen floor (that will give the kids something to think about!), I instinctively knew that I was not going to laugh.

"My dog, Ben, a Labrador cross," Mr Cliffe continued, "will not allow either me or the wife out of the house," he paused, "we got him from a shelter six months ago. At first we thought we had got ourselves a bargain, and then a few weeks ago this started to happen," he sighed audibly.

I knew straightaway where Harry and his dog Ben were coming from, I told him that this was a common problem and that it could be dealt with quite easily. When I arrived at Mr. & Mrs Cliffe's house, I was greeted quite affably by Ben and he conducted himself like a perfect gentleman. He fussed me but did not go overboard. The layout of the house was tailor-made for Ben, the front door opened into the living room, that led straight through into the dining area and then a door lead into the kitchen, in between the two rooms was an open staircase.

Once I sat down, Ben settled himself at a vantage point, which was on a landing halfway up the stairs. The house lent itself perfectly for Ben's little display of dominance. So we put it to the test.

Mrs Cliffe stood up and went to put on her coat. Ben was off his mark like Flash Gordon and by the front door before her arm was in the sleeve of the coat. She walked towards the front door and Ben growled and grumbled at her preventing her from trying to leave the house, she could not even reach for the door handle. Whilst this was happening, Mr Cliffe got up and walked to the back door as if to leave, when the dog noticed this, he left his post at the front door and shot off to try and secure the other exit, which then enabled Mrs Cliffe to leave the house.

When they had both gone the dog started to attack the back door with such ferocity that I thought it would do itself some damage. The dog was not in the least bit bothered by the fact that I, a total stranger, was sitting in the living room. Its only problem was coping with the fact that its underlings had left the house without his permission.

Although the action may appear extreme and can be quite frightening when witnessed, it is like most things with dogs, not always as bad as it looks. This show of destruction should be not misinterpreted for over-bonding. Over-bonding or separation anxiety, as some people call it, is manufactured by different means. Chapter 6 – Over-bonding, will explain all.

Back to Ben. I explained to the Cliffes the discipline Ben needed to put him right and left them to it.

Within two weeks Ben was no longer anxious about the Cliffes leaving the house; they could go out and leave Ben quite happily holding the fort until they returned.

CHAPTER 12
OWNING MORE THAN ONE DOG

One thing you can say about the British nation is that it is a lover of animals and I know that what we see on some television programmes does not always reflect this, but apart from the minority of people who are very cruel to their pets, whether by design or ignorance, on the whole we are very loving towards our pets, particularly our pet dogs, so it comes as no surprise that for one reason or another we find people who have a multi-pack of dogs in their homes.

In some respects it is good, as our shelters are bulging at the seams. There are always people who have a big heart and very little knowledge of what they are taking on – you might think that is a bit harsh, but it is true. When you hear those words from the shelter owner say, "Oh, he's back because they could not cope with the dog as he did not get on with their other dogs." I know there is something going radically wrong somewhere.

The tendency to have more than one dog is because they are pack animals and so people automatically presume that they will get on together, in some circumstances they do, to a point. It is hard enough to understand the workings of one dog without the added complication of throwing more into the mix.

Multi-packs do work – the trick is to know how to make them work.

There is always trouble bubbling under the surface and when it bubbles to the top, all hell breaks loose, it could be one dog or it could be more, who have the attitude that, I am the boss and it is done my way or no way. If you have one or more dogs with this approach then you have a major problem. But, like everything else, once you know where your dog is coming from you can understand where it is going, this way you can deal with the problem appropriately.

Discipline is the only way to teach a dog where the boundaries are and how not to cross them. (Chapter 14 – Discipline, will get you sorted) but even with this magical ingredient you also need to know what causes the problems initially. In a house with a multitude of wannabes you have to use the same principle as you would with a family.

In every functional family there is an order, a certain order that needs to be followed, otherwise anarchy will break out (for the younger reader to understand the word anarchy, look it up in the dictionary!).

All dogs are not the same, they all have a role to play in life, a role that they are happy with and can cope. Dogs have a ranking system that puts any one dog above or below or on an equal footing with another dog. The ranking system consists of a dominant dog, a middle rank dog and a lower rank dog. The middle ranking dog is usually an opportunistic dog, meaning give an inch and it will take a mile. The lower ranking dog is quite happy with its station in life and has no interest in getting to the top. The rank of the dog has nothing to do with either the size or the breed. You can have a Yorkshire Terrier putting a Rottweiler in its place.

So now we have a house full of dogs, that on the surface seem to get along quite well together, then we introduce another member to the pack. The golden rule to remember is that the last dog in is not necessarily the underdog. So whilst the ranking system is being reshuffled we do not interfere. Dogs are like water they will find their own level. There may be a few scuffles along the way but unless it gets out of hand the less involvement we have, the sooner they will sort themselves out.

If things do not naturally drop into place then we have the rankings wrong. We need to be able to distinguish the top dog from the others. We do this by watching the actions of the dogs. You will notice that the lower ranks will allow the dominant one to go through small spaces first, for example, doorways, or to let it eat first or wait until it goes to its bowl. Simple things like these you will notice. Also you will see that the lower rank will display certain behaviour, it will avoid eye contact and lower its head and tail, trying not to get noticed, it is what we know as "keeping a low profile". The top dog will command all the best places to sleep, usually away from the rest of the pack. This dog should be treated according to its status. First with everything. The first hello in the morning and when returning home, the first food bowl down, even if there are only nanoseconds between the actions, this is enough. Respect the rank and you will not have any problems.

But, like most things there is always a drawback. Trouble comes from an unexpected quarter; the dominant dog starts to bully the underdog. Bullying is a common occurrence, it is not only confined to people, dogs do it too. It is not aggression in the actual meaning of being aggressive, some dogs turn it into a sport, they enjoy doing it and they do it because they can and if there is no one to stop it happening it will continue and make the other dog's life a total misery. It is at this point that the owners will misdiagnose the problem and drastic measures are taken.

Once you are aware of what is happening you will not be tempted to recycle either dog. The signs to keep an eye out for are; if the dominant dog is lying down or on its bed and the other dog happens to wander by, you will find the top dog will have a low grumble, or you may notice it stares at the underdog. The poor unfortunate dog will not want to get eye contact with it so it will slink away somewhere out of the line of fire.

Sometimes the top dog will leave a toy as bait and will lay in wait for the other dog to come along and pick it up to play and then trouble erupts, or it may leave some food in its bowl hoping the other dog will think it is not wanted, and that is when the dominant dog will pounce. I have known a dog to enter a room where the top dog is and then walk the perimeter of the room to find a spot to lie down rather than pass the other dog.

When you see these things happening you step in. When the dog grumbles at the other dog say "No." Always get eye contact with the dominant dog when saying "No." When you find it staring at the other dog you say "No," again. You are not interfering with the order of things you are effectively letting the dog know that you are aware of what is occurring and you, being the ultimate top dog, do not approve.

I have known some clients I have visited to have mesh doors installed into their homes so they can determine the whereabouts of one dog and they can escort another dog outside or to be fed or in some cases to take a dog for a walk. Some clients use cages to help them juggle their dogs around. In other cases even take their dogs for a walk individually, even when they have five or six dogs. There is no need to go to such lengths to keep their dogs apart, doing this is not the answer and it will only alienate them from each other and make a bad situation worse.

There are dogs on the other end of the scale that will squabble terribly between themselves and then sleep quite blissfully together at night cuddled up on the same bed but during the day fight like cat and dog. Usually the spark which ignites this kind of behaviour is the presence of the owner. The dogs clamour to attract their owner's attention causing disruption in the household. This happens because the owner has no control over the dogs and so they perceive the owner as the weak link in the ranking system.

I have, throughout this book, constantly referred to getting to grips with any situation regarding the owners having total control over their dogs, whether it is with one dog or twenty dogs. Without discipline you do not have a hope. Respect is gained by being firm but fair, no treats, trickery or coercion will solve the problem. We owe it to the dog/dogs we take on to give them a good life, to make up for their bad start, which most of them have had, to help them enjoy life, to love them, but above all to understand them.

CASE HISTORY ONE
OWNING MORE THAN ONE DOG

I was called to visit a customer's home as they had a problem with some of their dogs. They were becoming dominant towards them and the other dogs. Considering they had about ten dogs, it was hardly surprising that they had concerns at one time or another.

It had been, according to the owners, quite a happy household until these particular individuals decided to cause trouble with the rest of the pack.

In some families, I have found this kind of problem tolerable and tolerable is as good as it gets. Juggling is what the uninitiated are good at, but the reality of it all is that, at the end of the day, it will wear you down and at some point you have to admit defeat. It was at such a point that I was called out to some very frustrated owners to make sense of some very famous dogs.

When I arrived at the palatial home I was confronted with a wave of the most beautiful Labrador puppies I have ever encountered. They were, without a doubt, "blonde bombshells". I was also aware of the atmosphere between the dogs, which was very tense. The parents of the young upstarts were amongst the dogs who were not getting on so well.

It does not necessarily follow that the parents are the ones the rest of the family have to follow. Younger members of the same family can be more dominant than their parents. Sometimes the kids can, and do, outrank mum and dad and this is what was happening in this home. The trouble was caused by the owners not understanding the ranking system dogs have and this can be a fatal mistake. Knowing what to do and understanding how things work, these problems can always be put right.

The owners were following what they thought should be the pecking order from the parents down, all the way to the last puppy born, obviously they had got it wrong, so disharmony was disrupting the happy band of thespians for awhile, but harmony has now been restored.

CASE HISTORY TWO
OWNING MORE THAN ONE DOG

Over the years I have answered the telephone to many people who are hoping to whip (not literally!) their wayward pets into shape. They ring with a certain amount of confidence that their dog's problems can be put right. Their main concerns are the usual ones, how long will it take and how much will it cost.

Then I get the telephone call from a distraught person who actually gets very upset on the phone when they are trying to explain their particular problem to me and they are under the impression that they are in the last chance saloon and know deep down nothing can be done.

It therefore gives me great pleasure to be able to tell them that the problem they are suffering from can be put right. I also get a buzz when I save a dog from a miserable existence, and one such dog among thousands, was a dog called "Cuddles".

When I arrived at the house I was taken into a very large room with floor to ceiling windows, half a dozen sofas and a giant open fireplace with a roaring fire. I sat at one side of the fire, the owner, Helen, sat at the other. Draped across the sofas, were eight dogs of all shapes and sizes, makes and models. In between Helen and myself, practically roasting, was Sam, the dog I had come to sort out.

Helen told me that she had had Cuddles the longest, long before Sam and she did not think that it was fair that Sam was making Cuddles life a misery. All the other dogs were quite happy with the way things were.

Helen naturally wanted it to stop but did not know how to do it. She did not even realise that the problem could be resolved without getting rid of at least one of them. Cuddles was so despondent and looked to be losing weight. It was then she knew something had to be done.

I asked Helen what she had been doing to put things right. She told me she had started to try and protect Cuddles by telling Sam off and putting Sam outside or into another room. She said Sam did not necessarily bother with any of the other dogs, he would pick on them if he felt like it and they would just walk away and settle down somewhere else. The owner never got to interact properly with them all when Sam was about because he always wanted to be there before anyone else and soon grumbled to let the others know.

Whilst we were sat there, the scene was set, Cuddles came into the room, he was a long haired German Shepherd and was beautiful and worthy of his name. The second he saw Sam he would normally have left the room, but because this was stage managed, Cuddles had no choice. He walked all the way around the room, Sam's eyes never left his face as he watched the dog slink round the outskirts of the room and then he settled down in the furthest corner he could find, not daring to come to his mistress for the cuddle he craved.

Helen's first mistake was to punish Sam by telling him off and then putting him into another room. As I have mentioned before, the top dog gets the top dog status, it does not matter how old or how long you have had the dog, it is the ranking of the dog which matters the most. But it was obvious that Sam was bullying him and all the others to a degree. He was not only top dog over the others, he was top dog over Helen and was slowly but surely segregating her from the rest of the pack.

You will be pleased to know that Helen followed instructions and everything is hunky-dory and Cuddles is enjoying his namesake.

CHAPTER 13
NERVOUSNESS

Some dogs do not receive the best start in life which can cause them to become frightened of their own shadow and very nervous of everything around them. This can be put right through correct training, it does not have to be the end of the world, the dog can live a happy, stress free life.

When a dog is born it either gets on or it could fall by the wayside. If it is a dominant puppy it will survive through fair means or foul. If it is a middle ranking puppy it will get there in the end. A low ranking one will get what it is given and make the most of it, usually surviving by ducking and diving and, some, not all, can leave the nest with some anxiety. If the puppy meets a family who feeds its insecurities instead of getting to grips and sorting it out then the poor puppy will not live a happy and fulfilled life.

Buying a puppy from a breeder at eight weeks old is important as this way we know it is well balanced, before eight weeks it is too soon to be taken away from its mother, and the same nervousness can occur if the dog is left too long with its mother. The best puppies are those who have been brought up in a house where it will be quite at home with the normal noises of a busy happy household, which should contain the noises of vacuum cleaners, washing machines, (and I thought I would never say this), screaming children running about, in fact all the usual sounds. If this is the case then nothing should surprise the puppy and it will act favourably to these noises. If this is not the case then it will respond quite differently. If a puppy shows any signs that it is afraid of anything then the first response of some owners is to try and protect the puppy. A puppy does not need protecting it needs to be able to come to terms with its fears.

Dogs, as we know, are there to protect us and its territory. It would not be doing much protecting hiding under the dining room table shivering and hoping that someone will come along and help. Therefore, when we get involved we look at the situation through our perspective and not the dog's. For example, if the dog comes across say a carrier bag caught in the hedge bottom, and the dog shows signs of unease, we pull it away. The best thing to do is to allow the dog to sniff the bag. We know it is not going to hurt the dog, so let the dog make up its own mind, do not make it an issue.

If your dog is frightened of traffic do not take it where there are many passing lorries or cars, choose a route where you will meet very little traffic. If you are near a busy road try and walk the dog at a quieter time of day, this way you are not throwing your dog in at the deep end. We want the dog to get used to traffic, but in small doses. If your dog is small do not be tempted to pick him up, if he hides behind your legs leave him there, do not speak to him and do not force him into a situation where he cannot cope, it will never work, the dog has to find its own way of coping without being stressed.

If your dog is nervous of people in the street just keep walking. If you meet someone you know and wish to stop and speak, make your dog sit, and then ignore him.

When in the house with visitors and the dog looks as if it is bothered, ask your guest not to make eye contact with the dog and ignore him totally. Eventually he will slowly but surely creep closer to the visitor, but still no eye contact. Some dogs show their nervousness by barking at the visitor then running towards his owner. The owner should not stroke the dog in a misguided attempt to calm him; the dog will not see this as being calmed but as a reward for acting aggressively towards someone in the house.

Another side to a dog's anxiety for some owners is trying to get the dog to go outside late at night because it is scared of the dark. People go out with their torches and their wellies in bad weather and there is no need as we actually make it worse for ourselves by the ridiculous things we are prepared to do to make life easier for the dog and at the end of the day we are not doing them any favours.

In certain cases a dog acting a little nervous is very beneficial for him as some dogs learn that if it is asked to respond to a command and he visibly shakes, the owners feel sorry and fuss the dog. Then the dog learns if it shows signs of being upset or cowers or adopts a submissive posture, the owners will fuss him. Some shelter dogs have succeeded in getting this off to a fine art.

Another no-no is not to turn a dog's rejection into a phobia. For example, putting him outside when it is raining, "Oh, he does not like rain for some reason." Or another classic, "He hates the French doors and will not come in through them, (although he will go out that way). When I ask him to come in he will as far as the doors, but will not come through them. I have to bribe him with a biscuit." You would be surprised how many owners have fallen for that one!

If you instil discipline the moment the dog steps over the threshold, regardless of age and where you have acquired him from, all these little foibles would never come to the surface.

CASE HISTORY ONE
NERVOUSNESS

Nervousness in the wrong hands can have an adverse effect on a dog. I was asked to go and see Mr and Mrs Beckett but before I could make an appointment, I can say without over exaggerating, I was verbally grilled before I could persuade them that I was just what they were looking for. To be fair to the Becketts they had had a bad experience.

Their two year old Boxer, called Petal (don't ask!), was bought from a breeder but because the dog's mother did not take too well to her puppies, the breeder sold them at an early age. Petal was only six weeks old when the Becketts brought her home. The cards were stacked against Petal from the beginning, she was loved and protected because of her poor start in life, which in a way is a natural instinct to protect a young animal, but it does not always pan out the way we expect. The Becketts realised that Petal was not developing properly, she

was literally ducking and diving at her own shadow and would not leave their side. Every visitor was a mammoth threat. Some months later it became apparent they had made a big mistake, although they thought they were doing right, they eventually realised they were not doing Petal any favours.

They booked a dog trainer to come to the house and sort out the problem. Firstly, the trainer tried to make friends with Petal by forcing her attentions on the dog, but all she managed to achieve was to back Petal into a corner, literally, and force eye contact, which Petal did not like, and according to the Becketts, Petal started to grumble low but insistent, in fact in their own words, Petal was quite menacing. The trainer was not put off and continued on her ill-fated commission. She took no notice of Petal's early warning system which Petal emanated before she was forced to protect herself. The trainer then proceeded to commit the classic schoolgirl error. She explained to the Becketts that getting down to the dog's level was the way to go, but Petal had had enough of this amateur, she bit her on the nose.

CASE HISTORY TWO
NERVOUSNESS

"Hello, is that the dog trainer?"

"Yes", I said.

"Well I am Mrs White and I have a little Westie called Ben. He has a phobia about lights, and we do not seem to be able to help him. He is afraid of the car lights which go past our cottage at night, the lights from the cars sweep across the sitting room ceiling and it really upsets him. He jumps around barking every time one goes by and we have no idea how to deal with it," she said.

"Is it just car lights or any light?" I asked.

"It's any light, when we put the ceiling light on to disguise the car lights he barks and barks until we switch it off, we just can't win."

I asked her a few more questions then we made an appointment for me to visit. Mrs White was most insistent that I called at night so I could see how troubled he was. I did not

The moral of this story is, you do not make eye contact, because eye contact is a direct threat and you never go down to the dog's level because we are not on a dog's level.

Fortunately this case had a happy ending.

need to go at night because I knew exactly what Ben was doing and why.

It is not in dispute that Ben's initial reaction to the lights was him being unsure of what they were. It is the response of Mr and Mrs White towards Ben's so called phobia which has made a mountain out of a mole hill.

Firstly, Ben has picked up on the fact that when he saw the lights he would bark and the lights went away. In his mind that is how it worked, something similar to the postman, he comes to the house every day and every day the dog barks and the postman goes away. As far as the dog is concerned the postman has gone because the dog barked at him.

This is a lesson on how not to turn a dog's insecurities into something bigger. If the Whites had had more control and more understanding of Ben they would have nipped it in the bud the first time Ben barked at the lights. Because they had misunderstood they made a fuss of him every time he barked. They believed they were calming him but the exact opposite was true. Therefore when they put the ceiling light on he barked and they turned it off, Ben was enjoying all the attention whilst Mr and Mrs White continued to endure miserable evenings.

CHAPTER 14
DISCIPLINE

Discipline – what does it mean? The dictionary tells us that it is a control or order exercised over people or animals. A system of rules used to maintain control.

This is the exact way I train dogs. I do not coerce them, bribe them, beat them into submission, trick them or use any kind of gadget whatsoever and it is not done by mirrors.

When we think about getting a dog there are a few questions we need to ask ourselves and one of them is: what do we want from our dog? We want to be able to walk the dog properly on a lead without it pulling. We want the dog to respect us and other people, we also want it to react friendly towards other dogs and animals (including cats!), respect our children and other people's children.

When the dog enters our home we have a duty not only to the dog but also the people who come into contact with him, therefore we need to have ground rules if we expect from our dog all that is listed above and more.

When I visit someone's home to help them with their dog they are usually under the impression that their dog has only one problem. For example; he will not come off the furniture or he will not come back when called. What they do not know is there are several problems which need to be addressed before you can stop the dog from jumping on to the furniture and getting it to come back when called.

There is only one way to successfully sort out all the dog's behavioural problems and that is to get to the root of the problems which lie with the owners. Educating them about how to train their dog and then everything will fall into place. To be fair to most owners they are bombarded by bad advice.

At this point I will clear up a few misconceptions I am often asked about things I have witnessed people doing to let the dog know that the owner is the boss. Some owners tell me that they do not fuss their dog when they meet in the morning or when they come home. They have been told somewhere along the line that it is not the thing to do and they find it hard to comply. Dogs have been greeting their pack members for hundreds of year so why stop what is inherent in the dog. How is the dog supposed to understand just because we cannot get it right?

Other non-starters are about toys. Dogs should be able to amuse themselves but should have access to their toys. It is bad advice that you only bring out the toys when you want to play with the dog. Going through a door before the dog and having your meal before he does and pretending to eat out of the dog's bowl before you put it down (what's that all about!). All these things do not make a blind bit of difference if you do not have discipline in place, and if your dog is disciplined then you would not need to do it.

Dog training should not rest on foolish conjecture, it should be taken seriously. To get our dog to comply we have to give it commands. Commands he understands the moment they are issued, they have to be quick and concise, too many words will go straight over the dog's head. You have to be quick to react to the dog the second it steps out of line. Every command you give your dog must be obeyed. The dog should never ignore an instruction. If you ask a dog to sit, then sit it must. If your dog will not obey by a verbal command then you have to get

physical. Place your hand on the back end and push gently into the sitting position and tell him to stay, if he moves, put him back.

The dog does not want to be confused by having more than one person issuing commands at any one time. The person who starts the command must see it through. Wives will often say to me "The dog will not do a thing I tell it, it will only listen to my husband."

The reason for this is because the wife tries to get the dog to sit and he totally blanks her and then the husband makes him sit. The dog now sees the wife as the weak link and he is less likely to obey her the next time because she did not enforce the command, someone else did.

It is not one person in the family who should train the dog, everybody must have a say then the dog will respect all members of the family. A four year old should be able to make the dog sit and stay.

Now to put your command skills into practice. Most dogs have a bed, but they are used for the wrong reasons. A dog's bed should be put down at night time when the dog goes to bed, or when you have visitors and you do not want the dog jumping up at everybody and making a nuisance of itself, and you do not want to put him away in another room on his own. For this next exercise you can use the bed as the focal point. If you do not have a bed anything similar will do, an old towel or sheet. Another way of getting an un-receptive dog to obey, is to put his bed down in a room where you are sitting, perhaps watching television, somewhere away from you and get the dog to go and sit in his bed. This is a good test to let you know how much control you have over your dog.

I always ask the owners if their dog will readily get into his bed "Oh yes," is the reply.

So we put it to the test, they bring in the bed and put it down and then tell the dog to get into his bed, the dog looks at them and walks away. "I cannot understand that," most of them state. The answer is simple enough, the dog will get into his bed when it wants but it is another matter entirely when you actually tell the dog to get into his bed. Therefore because you have asked him to do something you must follow it through. If he does not get onto the bed when told then you get the dog by the collar and make it. The object of this exercise is that the dog has to do what it has been told. If you ask him to get into his bed, then he must. The dog has to stay there for ten minutes, if he gets out, you put him back. It soon becomes a battle of wills but there can be only one victor and that has to be the owner. Each time you put him back the clock starts again. He may get off the bed fifty times but you put him back fifty-one times. When the ten minutes is up you call the dog to you and make him sit, when he does you give him five seconds of fuss and then ignore him. If the dog refuses to come to you then you must go and fetch him out. If he comes out of the bed but does not sit then he goes back for two minutes not ten. Then go through the process again until he comes to you on the first call. Whilst the dog is on its bed you should be able to go outside, upstairs etc. and the dog should still be on his bed when you get back. If the dog is on his bed when members of the family arrive home, he should not get off his bed to greet the newcomer, he should stay there until told to come off by the person who put him there. Do not let the dog go to sleep or the whole exercise is lost and do not exceed the ten minutes.

People ask me if the dog associates the bed with punishment. The answer is NO, all you have done is ask him to go on his bed. It is not a bed of nails and the dog is still in the same room as the owner. The reason for using the bed is, as I have said before, it is a focal point, so there is no mistaking where you want the dog to go. Do this as often as possible, when the ten minutes are up and the dog is off the bed then pick up the bed so the dog cannot get back onto it. It is important that you do not leave the bed down; it goes down only when you do the ten minutes, and at bedtime. It is worth noting at this point that if your dog sleeps in a cage then you must restrict access to it, the cage door should be closed during the day and opened only at night, when everyone goes to bed or when you leave the house.

In four days time, along with the other disciplines you will be undertaking, you will see a definite difference in your dog's behaviour. You will be surprised at how much respect you will have earned once you have mastered this task.

To keep the discipline flowing in the right direction, you now need to put right all the mistakes already made. The minute I knock on a client's door, I know the dog's life of Riley is about to come to an end. When I enter the house I notice that the dog is allowed on the furniture and settles down nicely. This is where the fun begins. Firstly, we need to get the dog down, so I explain that the dog must come off the furniture, eight out of ten people will say that is fine, but you find some who will say they don't mind him on there as it is an old sofa. Then I have to explain that it has nothing to do with the sofa, it has to do with the relationship between you and your dog. Your dog should not be on your level,

he will see himself as being on your level and this is wrong, it gives the dog the wrong idea.

Also, when I ask where does the dog sleep? I am informed that he sleeps in the bedroom with the owners, so he has to come out of the bedroom and sleep downstairs, yes he might complain, but he still has to go even if it is kicking and screaming. He will get used to it, ignore all the noises, it might be a good idea to have a word with your neighbours and explain what you are doing.

When people first start to put their foot down with a dominant dog, the dog quite naturally will grumble, he does not like his authority questioned by an underling. If you try to get the dog off your sofa and it tends to snap, which is only to be expected from a dominant dog when he is told what to do, rather than risk being bitten, put your dog onto a trailing lead, but only when you are in the house with the dog, never leave the lead on if you leave the house. This way you can get the dog off the sofa; just tell him to get down, if he refuses grab the end of the lead and pull the dog off, and repeat every time he jumps up. Dogs learn by association, each time he jumps up he will have to get down; he will soon get the message. This exercise should only take twenty-four hours to cure if you do it correctly. Now the dog is off the sofa and out of the top dog's sleeping quarters. Each step taken in the home reduces his high ranking status.

Another problem is when the owners are trying to settle down for the evening, the dog is constantly wanting their attention, whether it jumps up whilst they are sitting down, nose nudging their arm or bringing a toy to play which he either drops onto your knee or in front of you. You leave the ball where it has landed, both these actions must be ignored, do not look at the dog, do not speak to him, not even to tell him to go away. If he is pawing your arm, move it, or if he has both paws on your knees and it is in your face, put your hand up to protect yourself. The dog will be trying to get eye contact. You totally blank him, but do not be tempted to push him away. He will eventually receive the message that the attention he is looking for is not forthcoming and so he will get down. If there is more than one person in the room the dog will move on for their attention, but each person should ignore him.

Sometimes when a dog is being ignored he will be tempted to bark at the owners until they do something about it, even if you tell the dog to shut up he will have won, because you have given him the attention he was seeking. Once the dog realises that he is getting zilch, he will walk way and find something else to do, usually he will lie down. Only when the dog has been lying down and has not shown any attempt to attract your attention for at least an hour then you should call him over to you, make him sit by your side and then you can cuddle him for as long as you want, then you stop and go back to blanking him again. If the dog's last interaction was that it wanted to play then when the hour is up you pick up the toy and play for as long as you want. At the end of the game you make sure you have the toy and the game is over, putting the toy on the floor and walking away. As far as we are concerned we have played a game, the dog, however, sees it as a challenge, that is the difference, that is why at the end of play we have the trophy, it signifies to the dog we have won. Then you go back to blanking the dog. Your dog gets his cuddles and gets to play, but now it is on your terms and not his.

Feeding is another problem. When I see food down I always ask how many times a day do they feed their dog, and the answer is "I put it down in the morning, he does not eat straightaway, he isn't a greedy dog, he is a grazer, and I just fill up his bowl." Cattle graze, not dogs, it is bad practice to leave a dog's food down, it is like everything else, even the food is on tap. The bowl should be put down at a proper feeding time. The dog must be told to sit before he is fed. If the dog has not eaten his food within one hour, then the bowl is picked up and not put down again until the dog's next meal time. This way the dog understands that if he does not eat his dinner it will disappear. It is not long before he gets the message.

Another little annoying habit of an attention seeking dog is the constant way he will want to go out, we get up to let him out and two seconds later he wants to come back in again, then it is repeated again and again. This continues for some time until the owners get fed up, but they are never sure whether to risk not letting the dog out. The best way to get round this is to note the last time the dog actually did something and then you know it will not need to go for some hours. If he continues to roam around the room, call him to you and make him lie down and stay.

If your dog was from a shelter or anywhere else, the moment he steps into your home discipline must be the first priority. This way you do not have problems with destruction either through over-bonding or dominance. The world should continue to revolve around you and your way of life and not the dog's. He has entered your domain so he has to fit in with you. If you leave at nine in the morning and get back home at four in the afternoon, then the dog will soon know the routine. Dogs do not have any concept of time; a well balanced dog will sleep away the time whilst you are out. You can turn a dog around in two weeks, but you have to get the recipe right for this to happen. No short cuts or it will not work.

Along with your over the top dominant dog you can get a dog which is totally opposite, he shows signs of dominance but they are not so obvious. These are the dogs we spoil to the extent that we do not recognise them for what they are, the world revolves around these dogs, and they know it. When I ask the owners about their dog not barking when someone knocks on the door, the answer is nearly always the same "Oh, he's not a barker", they state, as if some breeds of dog bark and some do not. This is probably where the saying "Why have a dog and bark yourself," originates. These dogs spend most of their time lounging about in their baskets and are the type who easily turn into fussy eaters, and when a stranger walks into the house they just look at them and never bother to go up and find out who they are.

How do we achieve this phenomenon? Simply by putting him first with everything we do for him. First in the morning we feed him, then we take him for a walk and then he comes over for a fuss, which will not be as often as an attention seeking dog. He will while away his time by sleeping until he is next fed or walked. You would like to engage him in some kind of game, but he does not want to know. Over the years I have visited homes who have been burgled and the dog has not made the owners aware of Burglar Bill downstairs nicking the silver until they get up the following morning to discover their valuables have gone. How can we rectify this? The first thing to notice is that the dog does not get out of his bed to greet you in a morning, but you greet him. Therefore in the morning you walk past the dog, you do not speak to him, you open the door and let him out. The dog may refuse to go out, if he does you make him go and close the door behind him. Pick up his bed until bed time. These types of dogs are turned easily into fussy eaters. You put the bowl down and because he knows that food is available he will walk away and feed later. This attitude in the wrong hands gets worse. The owners decide that the dog does not like his food so they add meat to attract the dog, then the dog only eats the added ingredient and leaves the rest. The owner starts to panic because they fear the dog is not eating enough, so they start to feed him by hand. Now the dog is really on a winner. The golden rule of feeding is to put the food down, not adding anything to the bowl, and picking it up after an hour, No dog will starve as long as there is food about. Some dogs

can stick it out for up to four days, but you stick to your guns. Delay feeding your dog in a morning, leave it an hour or more, if that is possible. Then walk the dog later, do not be in such a rush to do his bidding, make him wait, cut out some of the walks for now, you can always add them later. When he does come over for a fuss, ignore him and call him over for a fuss later, when you decide to and not when the dog wants to.

There is nothing nicer than having a game of fetch, but you throw the ball and the dog does not want to know. A lot of people will say that the dog does not know how to play, it never shows any interest. He knows how to play, he just does not see why he should engage in an activity with the hired help. All these alterations you do will bring the dog down the pecking order.

What we need to do now is to understand how they think, put everything right which we have got wrong and start again. We now have the knowledge to turn them round so why not use it.

CHAPTER 15
OLD AGE

Old age – if we are lucky enough to get to it, old age can be just as pleasurable if there is someone to help it along and to make life just that bit easier. We can all benefit from love and understanding when life gets a bit iffy at a certain age. When we consider how independent we once were when we were younger, then the same applies to our pet dogs too.

There comes a time in their lives when they need help and reassurance and time soon flies, they go from independent to dependent in a blink of an eye, but the transition can be made easier with a little help from their friends.

If you stop and think what they have given us over the years, they have devoted themselves to us, protected us, our family and property and tried very hard to understand us under very extreme circumstances. Now it's payback time. Old age does not, like most things, just happen, it sneaks up on us. There are some tell tale signs we might pick up on,

but we might not and if we do we may not quite understand what is happening.

Therefore this chapter will try and inform you of some of the things to look out for. The first is you may notice the dog's confidence, if it is a high ranking dog its ranking slowly diminishes, only because of its age. When we train a dog properly we do not undermine its capabilities (which are hereditary) in any way, we only harness and control it, we do this by natural means which translates into discipline. If we have done this job correctly the dog's instincts will kick in at the right time and protect us. If we were to divert from disciplining the dog it would revert back to type.

You will probably find that the dog wants to go out more often than it used to, most male dogs stop cocking their legs because urinating is more of a need to, rather than a direct scent marking, some old dogs do not have the strength to stand on three legs. Also you will find that it does not want to stay out in the garden for longer than is necessary. He may bark at what you see as unnecessary but it will make the dog feel more secure.

Whilst you are out walking he will be more aware of the surroundings, he will show signs of unpredictability over things it once would not have given a second thought, especially at night, a noise in the dark, whether it is inside or outside, will upset him, something which is quite innocent and not what you would expect the dog to bother about.

They will bark more and sound quite aggressive to people who come calling who they know and those who they are not sure if they do know. Hearing and eyesight fade just like the rest of us, but they still try and maintain that they are still capable of protecting us, the extra barking gives them confidence. On the plus side they do sleep longer.

Some dogs become incontinent; this can be a difficult time for the owner. At night if you cover the sleeping area with waterproof sheeting and then put washable bedding on top, this works quite well. If you are lucky enough this might be all you have to put up with.

It is important not to chastise the dog; he would be greatly upset if it appeared that you had turned against him after all the years of a very close friendship. It is now time for us to protect them as they protected us.

CHAPTER 16
THE INTERNET AND OTHER SOURCES OF INFORMATION

When I am called out to people's homes regardless their dog's problems I always ask how they have been treating this, what techniques have they been using, because nine times out of ten I have to sort out the additional problems which have been created through the owners getting it wrong, before I can set to and sort out the original one.

I wish I had a pound for every time a client has said to me "You are my last hope, I have tried everything else." Life is made a lot easier when most of our problems can be solved simply by asking a question in the right place and receiving the help and advice we not only expect but deserve. If we have health worries we go to the doctor, car problems we go to a garage and if our pets our poorly we take them to the vets. Therefore when we find that we have a problem with our dog's behaviour, we turn to someone we think can help us.

Some of my clients have gone to classes where bribery is the order of the day. One client had a trainer come to the house because her dog pulled on the lead. She was told to pull the dog's collar far up its neck towards its head and walk with the dog's lead held up nearly choking the animal with its front paws barely touching the floor. She soon dispensed of his services. The man hadn't got a clue, no dog should walk like that, it was obvious to a blind man that it was wrong.

The majority of people have followed what they see on the television, distract the dog by putting pebbles in a plastic bottle and shake it at the dog when it misbehaves, or use a water spray. Neither works and Chapter 4 will explain why not.

The Internet, which as we all appreciate, is amazing, anything we need to know the first port of call is our computer and the Internet is where you can find the all the answers, or can we?

One of my clients got herself in a right pickle. She had problems house training her dog, she therefore consulted the computer and was told to put vinegar down on the kitchen floor to stop the dog messing on it. Doesn't work.

Another client was advised to buy a cage; this would stop the puppy messing on the floor. This is a very common misconception.

A gentleman told me that to assert his authority on his dog to stop it from being dominant, he was to push the dog to the floor on its back and hold it there, with one hand on the dog's neck to hold it down until it stopped struggling. He was also holding a bandaged hand where the dog had bitten him!

The trouble with advice is that the world and his wife have an opinion about dog training and they are all on the internet. I have scrolled through quite a few web sites on the most popular problems occurring and after a couple of hours I was losing the will to live. I was left with the impression that there is little wonder shelters are full and why people are cruel to their pets. They read what they are supposed to do and when that fails it never crosses the owners mind that the advice was a load of rubbish. Therefore they blame the dog for not responding the way they expected it to and this is when cruelty rears its ugly headd.

Some sites deal with each problem individually and advise what to do, others just want to sell you a book, or a gadget, or a shock collar, others go to great lengths to tell you nothing.

One site regarding puppy house training said, and I quote, "A puppy is never house trained completely until it is 6 months old, some breeds even later." This is not true. Also advice on toilet training, "Give your puppy frequent access to its toilet area preventing soiling in the house". Not true. "Use special treats". Bad idea. "Put your puppy on a regular timely feeding schedule, know when your puppy last eliminated, keep a diary". It is not rocket science, why do people make it so complicated, house training is a lot simpler than these bad examples.

Another popular problem with dogs is separation anxiety, or what I call over-bonding. Now this next site was good for a laugh. They suggested that "Take your dog for a long walk before you leave for any extended period to drain its mental and physical energy", or "Sometimes getting a second dog will help the dog cope with its human pack leaving it", and then goes on to say "If you successfully position yourself as the pack leader to the first dog he will help you teach the second one the house rules". In my opinion if you successfully position yourself as the pack leader to the first dog it would not be suffering from separation anxiety in the first place and there would not be a need to go to the great expense of buying another dog. I rest my case.

If you want to know how to house train your dog properly do not risk everything on what someone might know. Ask your vet, your local council, they have lists of the appropriate people. Some dog shelters will only be too happy to help or ask at your local library, local press. Try your community first you will be surprised at what it has to offer.

Printed in the United States
by Baker & Taylor Publisher Services